Psychoanalysis after Freud

This book draws on a number of Freud's lesser-known works to explore psychoanalytic perspectives on memory, mourning and repetition.

It is remarkable that Freud in his speculations on the human psyche often took his point of departure in an insignificant detail. It might be a lapse of memory or a detail in a piece of art. From here he uncovered the many layers of the psyche, its complex structure and the processing of meaning right to the limit of understanding. At this point, Freud's exploration encountered the unknown, an internal outland as difficult to acknowledge as the external reality. Freud did not invent the unconscious, but he demonstrated how it works. The unconscious according to Freud does not exist, but insists on making itself visible. The eleven essays in this book draw a picture of the critical humanistic thinking so characteristic of Freud. His concepts and suppositions were the result of many years' speculations, based on observation, experience and ideas, and although they are marked by the time and culture from which they emerged, they demonstrate a revolutionary knowledge of the psyche transcending the knowledge of his time. In her reading of the selected texts the author has chosen the position of a contemporary interpretation and has added her own after thoughts and critical comments.

Examining how psychoanalytic work on the topics of memory, mourning and repetition has changed since Freud and how these themes remain of crucial importance in contemporary psychoanalytic theory, this book intersperses theory with clinical practice. It will be of great interest to training and practicing psychoanalysts, as well as scholars of art, literature and sociology.

Judy Gammelgaard, professor, Dr. of Philosophy and psychoanalyst, has written a great many books and articles, some based on clinical experiences, while others are elaborations of psychoanalytic theory and concepts. She has for many years been especially interested in bringing psychoanalysis into dialog with literature, art and culture.

Psychoanalysis after Freud

Memory, Mourning and Repetition

Judy Gammelgaard

Translated by Maria Yassa

Routledge
Taylor & Francis Group

LONDON AND NEW YORK

First published in English 2022
by Routledge
2 Park Square, Milton Park, Abingdon, Oxon OX14 4RN

and by Routledge
605 Third Avenue, New York, NY 10158

Routledge is an imprint of the Taylor & Francis Group, an informa business.

British Library Cataloguing-in-Publication Data
A catalogue record for this book is available from the British Library

Library of Congress Cataloging-in-Publication Data
Names: Gammelgaard, Judy, author.
Title: Psychoanalysis after Freud : memory, mourning and repetition / Judy Gammelgaard ; translated by Maria Yassa.
Other titles: Efter Freud. English
Description: Abingdon, Oxon ; New York, NY : Routledge, 2021. | Includes bibliographical references and index. |
Identifiers: LCCN 2021005899 (print) | LCCN 2021005900 (ebook) | ISBN 9781032048628 (hardback) | ISBN 9781032046716 (paperback) | ISBN 9781003194880 (ebook)
Subjects: LCSH: Freud, Sigmund, 1856-1939. | Psychoanalysis. | Bereavement--Psychological aspects. | Memory.
Classification: LCC BF173.F85 G3413 2021 (print) | LCC BF173.F85 (ebook) | DDC 150.19/52--dc23
LC record available at https://lccn.loc.gov/2021005899
LC ebook record available at https://lccn.loc.gov/2021005900

ISBN: 978-1-032-04862-8 (hbk)
ISBN: 978-1-032-04671-6 (pbk)
ISBN: 978-1-003-19488-0 (ebk)

Typeset in Bembo
by MPS Limited, Dehradun

Contents

Introduction

The texts in this book all came into being as an afterthought. The point of departure was a selection of Freud's lesser known texts. From a contemporary perspective, I have added my personal comments and critical afterthoughts to these. As Freud's own writing has the character of afterthought, they point to the fact that the insights and realisations of the psychoanalytic process occur in afterwardness.

In my choice of texts from Freud's oeuvre, I have steered away from his theoretical works. They are doubtless important, but I have, favoured such texts that treat a subject, object or simple observation, for the reason that theory, in these texts, transpires in a vivid and lively manner, and because these texts do justice to Freud's open and questioning approach to what I have called the normal peculiarities of everyday life. The two first essays on transience and on memory depart from a well-known subject, with which most people are familiar. However, reflective afterthought reveals several layers of signification which are not evident at first reading. They are followed up by a text where Freud, on the basis of clinical experiences and his theorising on these, presents a short and condensed exposition of the relation between perception and memory. In the three following essays, Freud the clinician speaks about memory, mourning and repletion on hysteria and narcissism. I end up this clinical part of my book with a thorough examination of the idea of the symptom. The last four essays demonstrate how Freud widened the scope of psychoanalysis in his study of culture, civilisation, of war, love, art and literature.

Throughout his life, Freud strove to trace the reasons underlying psychic suffering and to develop a theory which could explain not only the reason and development of neurotic symptoms, but the life of the mind in general. He bequeathed a body of work built on surprising insights into the human psyche. Freud never intended psychoanalysis to be restricted to the treatment of psychical suffering in individuals. His passionate relationship to knowledge led him to ever new areas such as religion, mythology and art, in a continuous quest to uncover such phenomena that are not immediately meaningful. The most original and insightful results of Freud's scientific work were created in borderlands: on the border of the scientific recognition of his theory, on the frontiers of other research disciplines such as biology, philosophy, archaeology and linguistics and on the border of collective cultural phenomena such as re-ligion, art and literature. Curiosity and an unwavering conviction of the depths underlying the superficial and obvious led him to examine phenomena such as transience and disturbances of memory, and not least, to pursue dream life to the limits of the knowable. Here, he encountered that around which everything revolves, namely the unconscious. Freud was not the first to use the concept but it was he who theorised the unconscious as accessible to a certain form of ex-ploration but nevertheless as belonging to the unknown and invisible. The unconscious does not exist – but it nevertheless insists, and it was probably this insisting mode of revealing something in seemingly insignificant, fleeting and transient phenomena that was Freud's source of inspiration.

On one of the moments where he most penetratingly pursues the particular logic of the unconscious and of the drives is in his epochal and difficult text *Beyond the Pleasure Principle*. More than anywhere else, the unconscious is here revealed as inaccessible and incomprehensible. Reading this text gives a clear sense of some-thing steering Freud's exploration, and in the same degree, forcing it into the domains of the accessible and understandable. In my opinion, Freud's work should be judged and valued for the particular form of thinking that characterises it, and which evolved from the nature of the thing or condition under study. Realising that the object of his research was not immediately accessible, he saw the necessity of speculation. Freud was a speculative thinker, one could say, but nor primarily abstract. His point of departure was always an observation, which could not, however, be immediately grasped. To understand the deeper, inaccessible layers behind what could be observed, speculation was necessary. It came to characterise Freud's method of work, that he was untroubled by leaving behind unresolved observations and assumptions, or by adhering to earlier theories which, although replaced by new ones, to his mind remained to some extent valid. Freud's thinking is, in other words, refreshingly open to and accepting of the many contradictions he discovered in the hidden strata of the mind. Despite his resolve to maintain a sober and distanced stance to the objects of his study, he was forced to admit that this could not be done. In one of his case histories he writes that whoever calls upon the demons of the unconscious mind must be marked by them. In his writings on various subjects he conceded to the impossibility of remaining ob-jective, as the object under study is bound to influence the representation of it. Something in the very nature of the object under scrutiny, writes Freud repeatedly, will inform the writing process, as if possessing a will of its own.

This openness to the many peculiarities of the life of the mind, and the unfinished character of many of Freud's works are an inspiration to further thinking. I regard myself and my colleagues as heirs and followers, and it is in this light that the following should be read.

I have wished to render some of Freud's, to my mind, simultaneously charming, profound and serious texts, and to link them to my personal con-siderations and critical comments. I have, like Freud, allowed myself to be informed by literature and philosophy to the extent that these have enriched psychoanalytic considerations. It is a pleasure to read Freud's texts, as these, despite their complicated subject matters, are written in a beautiful, both articulate and understandable language. This has doubtless left its mark on my texts, despite my intention of making them accessible and understandable.

In the writing of this book it became clear to me that there are three themes: remembering, mourning and repetition, which recur in several texts. In the earliest days of psychoanalysis, remembering was understood not only as a function of the psyche, but as its very essence, and in early work on hysterical patients, Freud stated that these patients suffered from reminiscences or memories. These memories, however, were not consciously accessible. Rather, they were traces of memories, although actively working traces, one could say. It is no coincidence that Freud used the term *work* for several psychic processes and spoke of the work of remembering, the work of mourning and the work of dreaming. During sleep, a layer of the mind opens which is unknown to our waking life. Impressions and thoughts are transformed into visual images, experienced at the borders of waking life as moods, that at times colour several hours of the following day. The dream has accomplished psychic work, and effected an expression, in its own way, of feelings and wishes unresolved in waking life.

The work of remembering and the work of mourning share features with dream-work and are, as will be shown in the following, two sides of the same thing. Crucial to all three forms of work is the creation of links to levels of psyche where feelings and impressions, hidden from conscious life with its verbal and rational modes of thought, are revealed through other forms of expression than those of conscious life. Repetition, on the other hand, cannot be considered psychic work.

Psychoanalysis has taught us to differentiate two forms of repetition. There is repetition where what we repeat are certain themes and patterns, often beyond our awareness, and then there is the form of repetition which aims at nothing besides repetition itself. Freud called the kind of repetition he found in severely traumatised patients the repetition compulsion. Traumas were repeated in actions and dreams without bringing neither relief nor understanding. In repetition of the identical kind one mostly has the impression that repetition functions as a primitive warding-off of the catastrophic nature of the trauma.

Immersion in the inaccessible and often destructive aspects of the mind might have led to a pessimistic world-view. The texts in this book, despite the seriousness of their subjects, are not characterised by pessimism. To my mind, psychoanalysis is best described as illusion-critical realism combined with an open and sincere interest in everything human. Psychoanalysis is a human science, but it has a critical perspective on humanity, a critical perspective which is implicit in my reading of Freud.

Many thanks to my translator psychoanalyst, Maria Yassa, for her meticulous work and for the fine collaboration we have had during the whole process of translating.

Gl. Holte, November 2020
Judy Gammelgaard

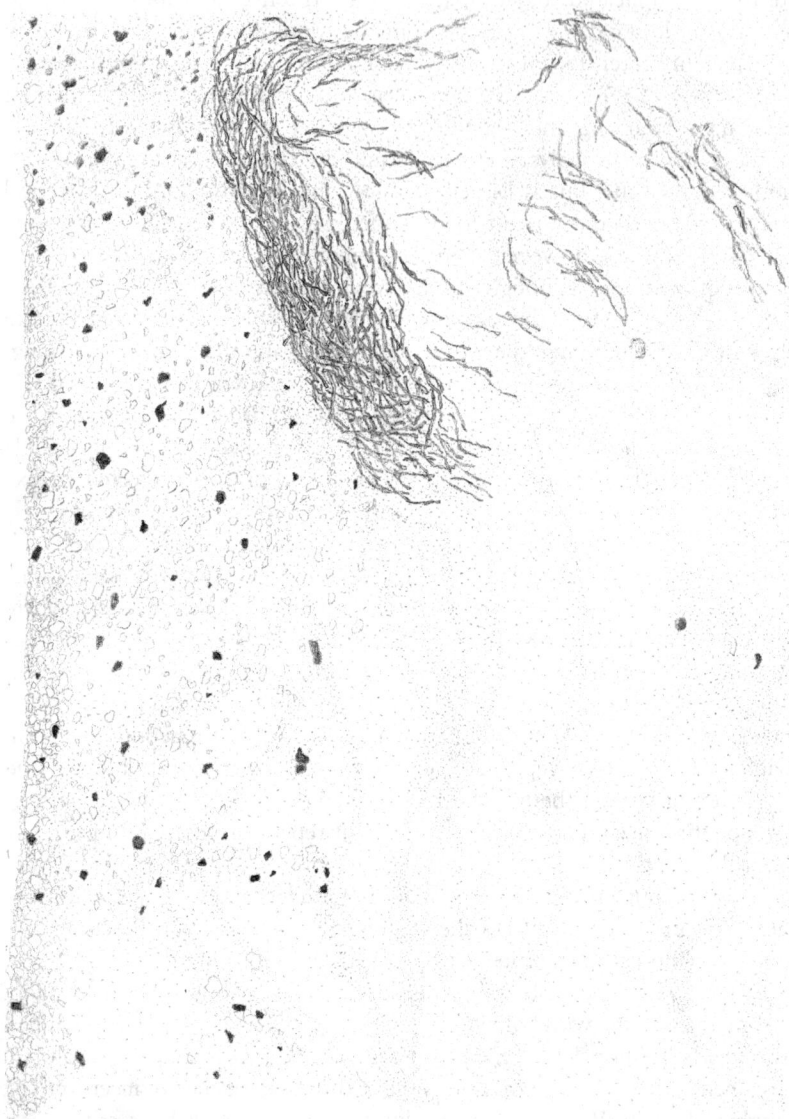

Chapter 1

On transience

In the late summer of 1913, Sigmund Freud was walking through a blossoming summer landscape in the company of a "young, but already famous poet" and a "taciturn friend". While admiring their surroundings, made even more beautiful by the soft light of the setting sun, their conversation took a melancholy turn. The young poet was haunted with sadness. Although appreciative of the beauty of nature, he was unable to free himself from the thought that all this blossoming beauty would disappear with the winter, just as all human beauty, and beauty itself was transient and doomed to wither and die. Looming in beauty was thus a touch of its inevitable decay, which prevented the poet not only from enjoying it, but also from finding any meaning in it. While the taciturn friend seemed to share the poet's view, Freud could not accept so pessimistic an outlook. His experience had taught him that there are two different reactions when individuals sink into despair faced with the transience of beauty and perfection.[1]

Some individuals can, like the young poet, succumb to painful melancholy, while others are inclined to oppose the reality of transience and to reject its inevitability. It can't be that all this glory is doomed, it is said. It is both meaningless and presumptuous to think thus. Beauty is eternal and will always withstand destruction, goes the reasoning behind this view. This claim to eternity, says Freud, is nothing but an expression of our wishful thinking, which refuses to submit to the inevitability of reality. Pain itself, he argues, contains an element of truth. The idea that beauty would be exempt from the transience of all things must be rejected as a reflection of our dreams and wishes. But need we, admitting the eventual decay of all things, fall into such despair that filled the mind of the poet with heavy thoughts? No – on the contrary, is Freud's answer. We could ascribe even greater value to beauty when realising that it is transient, and like life itself, finite. Spring, summer and a world in bloom will always follow the withering and decay of winter.

The human body and face, as well, lose their beauty but are no less treasured. This is also the case for works of art and the accomplishments of human rationality. Their value does not diminish for not being eternal. It is possible that a time will come when the art and culture we know will no longer exist, or might not be understandable and valued, and there might come a time when all life on earth is extinct. But, concludes Freud, attempting to convince the poet and their common friend, new beauty and new species will emerge, and not least, joy in the face of beauty is not dependent on its permanence but, on the contrary, on its fleetingness. These views, however, did not impress Freud's companions. Their resistance to his optimism in the face of the impermanence of all things gave Freud occasion to reflect on the reason for this. When it is impossible to enjoy beauty, and despair over its transience takes over, it is due to a lacking ability to mourn, he postulated. He had had the opportunity to study the work of mourning, as it is called in psychoanalysis, and the pain bound to it, both on a personal level and as a step in the development of psychoanalytic theory.

Freud's essay on transience was not written at the time of the walking tour, which took place in the late summer of 1913. Two years later, he found reason to write his essay, when receiving an invitation to participate in a "Festschrift" celebrating his absolute literary ideal, Goethe. It is also doubtful whether the walking tour actually happened, or if it was a literary fiction used by Freud as a frame for his narrative on transience. He chose to conceal the identities of his two companions. These have later been revealed as Rainer Maria Rilke and Lou Andreas-Salomé.[2] Freud had indeed had a conversation with the poet and the "taciturn" friend in 1913, but it did not take place in the summer landscape in which Freud set it, but in a hotel lobby in Munich, in connection to the fourth psychoanalytic congress, attended by Rilke and Lou, for different reasons – Lou, because she was part of the inner circle of the psychoanalytic association, and Rilke, because he was ridden with internal torments which inhibited the creative resources that were vital to him. Rilke had on several occasions attempted to begin analysis with Freud, but had never followed through. Like many artists, he feared analysis would stifle the source of his creativity, despite it also being the source of his numerous and serious torments. Lou, herself an analyst, shared his view and dissuaded him from analysis. Rilke paid Freud a final visit the year that Freud wrote his essay, and on this occasion clearly expressed his relationship to psychoanalysis in stating that no lasting bond between him and psychoanalysis could be forged. In other words, the commitment inherent in undertaking psychoanalysis was repelling to him. There were probably several reasons for this.

The conversations with Rilke and Lou must have made a lasting impression on Freud, as he, a couple of years later, used a completely different occasion to write down his thoughts and reflections on a subject with which he was deeply preoccupied, and which contained one of the paradoxes that stimulated and nourished the development of psychoanalytic theory. Something in these conversations escaped his comprehension, something which two years later became all the more intrusive, as the world had burst into flames.

The walking tour with the poet occurred only one year before World War I erupted and destroyed the beauty of the landscapes and works of art. The war also left culture and its products in ruins, leaving the world in painful realisation of the destructive aspects of human nature, extinguishing the hope of the peaceful co-existence of humans despite national, ethnic and religious differences. When Freud wrote about the conversations with Rilke and Lou, war was a reality. It struck Freud on a personal level, as his two sons, Martin and Ernst, were sent to the front, and war made the question of mourning present and pressing. How do we recover from the loss of those we love, and how do we overcome – if at all possible – the enormous loss of human life, of meaning and hope, which war leaves us with?

Freud's little essay on transience raises interest not only because of the important subject it treats, but also because it was written, for Freud, in an unusually poetic style. The conversations with Rilke and Lou not only impressed him, but also sowed the seed of a disturbing idea, and compelled him to afterthought, which inspired him to render the conversations as a fiction set in surroundings far removed from the brutal reality which surrounded him at the time he wrote the essay.

Freud ends his beautiful essay by calling attention to the delay between the event and the afterthought – the delay so characteristic of psychoanalytic insight. We understand ourselves, whether in analysis or living our lives, retroactively, in the form of such memories that come to us, often beyond our conscious will.

My guess is that the conversations with Rilke and Lou not only clarified Freud's thoughts on mourning. The essay also points to something inherent to his person and work. I shall return to this after looking at the contribution of psychoanalysis to mourning and its work.

It is not surprising that we mourn the loss of a loved one or thing that has great value to us. On the contrary, this strikes us as a natural reaction, that we therefore do not think further about. In the same way that it does not occur to us to regard mourning as unhealthy, we take for granted that the mourner, after working through the loss, will regain vitality, and thus freed, turn towards the world. Psychologically, however, the phenomenon of mourning entails greater complexity.

I wonder if not most people would say that the capacity to feel love is innate, if only as a predisposition which develops and matures in relation to the people close to us. When love goes to pieces, or we lose a person dear to us, the loving feelings are withdrawn but will later be transferred to others, or they can be invested in creative activity or even in the subject's own ego. What is enigmatic about the process that analysis calls the work of mourning, and which consists exactly of love being withdrawn from the person who was the object of this love, is its duration and intense pain. Why does it take so long and hurt so much?

Mourning and its work can be clarified if we compare mourning with the condition that is called depression or melancholia. Unlike normal mourning, the depressive or melancholic has difficulty in terminating the work of mourning. In mourning and depression alike, love is withdrawn into the ego, and the object of love now exists only as an internal representation. Normal mourning consists in the mourner gradually assimilating the image of the lost object within him/herself, and in a way identifying with it, thus leading it to become part of the self. The mourner lives through a spell of time in the shadow of the lost object and accepts only gradually the brutal reality that demands that the loss be acknowledged, allowing the mourner the freedom to return to life. Normal mourning thus consists in a double process, where the mourner turns his/her back to life, draws the object into his/her ego, and in memory, conscious and unconscious, lives through the relation to the loved one. Through this work, the mourner can gradually, and not without resistance, accept the loss of the object without too much pain. For the depressive, this work fails for several reasons. It is as if the depressive was unable to free him/herself from the object, which remains as a shadow on the ego, with the result that the ego is depleted. The major difference between the mourner and the depressive is that whereas to the former the world appears empty and impoverished, to the latter the ego itself has become depleted, as it has lost itself in pain. This is expressed in the self-recriminations which are so characteristic of the depressive. The depressive subject deems him/herself unworthy and undeserving of love. The explanation of this difference between normal mourning and the depressive person who is incapable of accomplishing this work will be found in the nature of the relation that the person in question had to the lost object. Experience from therapeutic work has shown that regarding the depressive the relation with the lost object is characterised by unresolved ambivalence. At the moment of loss, the depressive is faced with the difficult task of mastering violent and often primitive feelings of rage, hate and love, and it is this ambivalent conflict that makes the work of mourning so difficult. The depressive can no longer address his/her accusations to an external object, only to the internal representation of this object. The depressive thus directs the negative feelings to parts of his/her own ego, which explains why depression is so painful and is for many depressives accompanied by thoughts of suicide.

The starting point of this account of the work of mourning was Freud's attempt to find an explanation to why the young poet was plunged into despair and melancholia when faced with the beauty of nature. Freud's assumption was, as we heard, that this must be a consequence of the inability to accomplish the normal work of mourning, with the concomitant acceptance that also beauty is transient, but precisely because of being transient all the more beautiful and precious. Was Freud's interpretation correct? When Rilke was unable to see blossoming beauty without being seized by despondency over its transience, should we see this as an expression of his inability to work through mourning?

Rainer Maria Rilke did not have an easy life. He came into the world in Prague in 1875 and was given the name René Maria Rilke. His Christian name, unspecific in gender, was probably due to Rilke's mother having wished for a girl. René was born barely one year after a sister had died, shortly after birth. As a child René was dressed in girl's clothes, and his mother let his hair grow long and called him "my little girl". In Rilke's novel on Malte Laurids Brigge is a passage where Rilke lets his narrator recount how he, as a boy, had guessed his mother's desire of his being a little girl. He had thus had the idea to knock on the mother's door, and when she asked who it was, he would joyfully cry out, that it was "Sophie", with a voice, "so dainty that it tickled my throat".[3]

Rilke was what one would call a replacement child – a child that is conceived as a consolation for the parent's loss of a dead child. The living child is thus inevitably identified with the dead one. Replacement children thus come into the world with an identity marked by death. This theme is present throughout Rilke's oeuvre from beginning to end, not only as a dreaded destiny, but also as an inspiring companion, a kind of aim for his artistic ambition. One carries, through the years, "deep inside his wallet, the account of a dying hour", he has his protagonist, Malte Brigge, say. Rilke had known anxiety for as long as he could remember. He lets Malte narrate how anxiety entered his life, at the time he was ill and feverish. Like a large, dead animal, it grew out of him like a tumour, and although he was quite small, the adults were unable to remove it.

Not far into the story of Malte Brigge, we are introduced to the novel's central theme of death, depicted through the death of Christian Detlev Brigge, the narrator's grandfather. "It was not the death of some poor wretch dying of a dropsy; it was the evil, regal death the Chamberlain had borne with him his whole life long, nurturing it from within himself. All those vast reserves of pride and will and mastery that he had been unable to use up himself in his calmer days had passed over now into his death, into that death which now presided at Ulsgaard, throwing it all away".[4]

Rilke suffered the anxieties and agonies of death. From the beginning of his life they became part of his character, as were the capacity and urge to create, and when he refrained from psychoanalytic treatment, it was probably for fear that it would endanger his creativity.

In 1897, Rilke met Lou Andreas-Salomé, who was to become his life-long friend, muse, mother and mistress. At Lou's instigation, he changed his name to Rainer Maria Rilke, and under her protection and guidance Rilke developed his love of art, language and music. In her, he acquired a confidante with whom he could share his thoughts and his art. Rilke never came to terms with the requirements of the real world. His crises and depressions were recurrent, particularly during those long periods when he was unable to write, and after a brief marriage, he lived in a state of chronic restlessness. Out of step with the world, he found himself in a permanent state of exile. It was after one of his depressive episodes that Rilke took Lou with him to Munich to meet Freud, and in 1915 he sought Freud one last time, in his home in Vienna.

With insight into Rilke's life history, anxiety and recurrent depressions, one cannot fail to follow Freud's thought, that Rilke was incapable of bringing the work of mourning to a resolution. But Rilke did not wish to lose that which his creative urge was made of. Rilke wrote on pain. His refusal of mourning and of the inevitability of loss had resulted in his escaping all relationships and finding refuge in poetry, which offered him temporary shelter from such demands that real life would have faced him with.

It is however not entirely true to say that Rilke was unable to mourn, as he, in his poetic oeuvre, was able to carry mourning into the sublime, to bitter-sweet melancholy. In his *Duino Elegies,* Rilke reveals himself as a master of elegy.

While the mourner eventually frees him/herself from the lost object and once again turns towards the world and towards new objects, the mourning of the poet is different. The poet does not free him/herself from the lost object, but in his/her pain finds the impetus for creative work, and in his/her art re-finds what was lost. In his *Letters to a Young Woman,*[5] Rilke explains that the key to artistic creation is to be found in that treasury of inexhaustible solace which is the work of art. This can only be witnessed in solitude, he wrote. It might be added that it is particularly the artist, who in his solitary creative process, can recognise the solace Rilke writes about to the young woman, and that he knew how to extricate from it a precious experience.

Marcel Proust has, like Rilke, insisted on letting the narrator of *Remembrance of Things Past* live through the emotional turmoil inherent in mourning. The author's narration of the beloved grandmother's death was to become one of the most beautiful testimonies that mourning, as embodied experience, not only mitigates grief, but also makes us rich in experience, in this case an experience which becomes the incentive to creative activity. In Proust, experience consists in the ability to link two impressions occurring at separate moments in time. The narrator arrives in the seaside resort of Balbec, accompanied by his grandmother. He retires to his room but finds no rest, in the hell of utterly strange surroundings, sleep becomes an impossibility. The grandmother comes to his help and bends down to unbutton his boots.

On the next visit to Balbec, the narrator is accompanied by his mother. The grandmother has died in the previous year. As the room, this time, is no longer terrifyingly immense, he calmly bends to remove his boots, and in the same moment, the reality of the grandmother's death strikes him. It is the identical action, which in a brutal fashion, brings back the earlier experience and creates a link between the presence of the living grandmother and the absence created by her death. The narrator elicits from this repeated action not only the loss of the reality that his grandmother was for him; he simultaneously experiences the loss of the self he was. This contradiction between the existing and its inexorable annihilation would be unbearable if it weren't for the numbing effect of time and habit. The narrator, however, will not be numbed. He transforms the spontaneously arisen pain into precisely that which his life's work will be written upon. "I knew that if I ever did extract some truth from life it could only be from such an expression at once so spontaneous, which had neither been traced by my intelligence nor attenuated by my pusillanimity, but which death itself, the sudden revelation of death, striking like a thunderbolt, had carved within me, along a supernatural and inhuman graph, in a double and mysterious furrow".[6]

Proust has his protagonist live through all the emotional shadings of mourning. The crushing experience of definitive loss confronts him not only with the opposition between the living and that which is forever lost, but also with the paradox that loss implies both guilt and compassion. As the dead remain alive within us, writes Proust, it is ourselves we strike when we remember the blows we have inflicted on them. And if we persevere in striking ourselves, it is because we can thus hold on to the relationship to loved and lost objects. The painful experience of mourning consists in living through all the emotions linked to the beloved and lost object without being able to find consolation and affection from the one object who could give it to us, but who is no longer present in our lives.

While Rilke could not relinquish the idea of death, which remained, clinging to the living, the narrator in Proust draws the conclusion that death is not in vain, as the dead remains within us, and act upon us even more forcefully than the living, since day-to-day life and the living veil the truth from us.

There is a sequence towards the end of *The Notebooks of Malte Laurids Brigge* which resonates with the theme Freud speculated upon in his essay on transience and which shows how the dead forever cast their shadow on everything alive. Malte addresses a series of fictive young women and asks them to look back into their diaries. Here, he says, they will find proof that spring is a time when the emerging year stands as a reproach, and they will be able to witness how despite the joy they might have felt, it was as if they had dragged the winter and the past year into the new one. And while they waited for their soul to take part in the new, it was as if their limbs became heavy, and something like a sickness invaded them, destroying their joyful anticipation.

In Proust we find a far more unambiguous joy over the budding spring. As a conclusion to the description of the many emotional facets of mourning, the narrator goes for a walk along the road on which he and his grandmother had often travelled. But while he, in the company of his grandmother, had only seen the leaves of the apple trees, the trees were now in full bloom "and hold aloft their pink and blossoming beauty, in the wind that had turned icy beneath the drenching rain: it was a day of spring".[7]

While Freud worked on his essay on transience, he quite clearly insisted on the joy of summer's blossoming beauty, but he wrote it at a time when the cannons of Europe laid villages and countries in ruins and spread death everywhere. He could probably not free himself from the poet's thoughts on everything's transience as a human condition. Human frailty appears against the background of the arbitrariness of war, as a brutal reality, which inevitably intruded on the joyful affirmation of life and its thriving. Freud might have felt the pessimism of the poet. As the scientist he was, he probably also found a certain satisfaction in offering his theory of unresolved mourning as a kind of explanation – and as a shield against falling into broodings upon what could not fully be explained.

Two years after the meeting with Rilke and Lou, Freud returned to their conversation, in the attempt of finding an answer to something that had disturbed him. In his essay on transience he writes that there are two attitudes to the phenomenon. One can, like the poet, fall into painful despondency, or one can defy the obvious. There seems to be a third position which Freud is not inclined to comment. One can use transience, with its characteristic of condition and necessity, as a creative force. Freud, like the poet, nevertheless knew such states of mind when the ability to write would not appear despite the pressing character of the subject. Freud knew, in other words, the creative process and the states of mind it implies, but had probably resisted and wished himself into the clear daylight where the scientist could triumph over dreamlike impressions and intuitive insights. In the letters to his friend Wilhelm Fliess, which served as first formulations of Freud's very first thoughts on the science he was developing, he writes about strange states of mind that were unavailable to consciousness, about vague thoughts followed by doubts penetrated only by weak rays of light. He also writes about his desire to immerse himself in Italian art, not from the perspective of art history, but as a preoccupation with absolute beauty, created from ideas rendered through space and colour, bringing joy to the senses.

Freud was preoccupied with art; he had delved into the pictorial arts and literature, and his writings testify to his urge to express himself with beauty and in accordance with that which his science sought to give answers to. But this inclination was also in contradiction with the truth, which he sought through his science and which could not tolerate too much mysticism. Although Freud mainly was rational and committed to his scientific method of work, he always admitted that there was something in the very object under his scrutiny which escaped stringent scientific method.

As we can see, Freud pointed to different attitudes to the transience of all things. We can choose to embrace pain, thereby risking to lose ourselves in it, or we can work through it and transform it into experience. Freud was inclined to choose the latter. He analysed the particular experiences he encountered in his personal life and made them a part of his utterly unique science. In his essay on transience he succeeded in giving literary form to his scientific investigation. Rilke was differently inclined. In answer to transience, he created a number of elegiac pearls of great beauty.

Notes

1 Freud, S. On Transience. *The Standard Edition of the Complete Psychological Works, Vol XIV*, pp. 303–309. London: The Hogarth Press.
2 Von Unwerth, M. (2005). *Freud's Requiem*. Mourning, memory and the invisible memory of a summer walk. New York: Riverhead Books. See also: Kristiansen, S. (2013). The psychoanalyst and the poet – a meeting between Sigmund Freud and Rainer Maria Rilke. *The Scandinavian Psychoanalytic Review*, 36 (1): 52–56.
3 Rilke, R.M. (1927/2009). *The Notebooks of Malte Laurids Brigge,* p. 64. London, Penguin Classics.
4 Rilke, R.M. (1927/2009). *The Notebooks of Malte Laurids Brigge,* p. 11. London, Penguin Classics.
5 Rilke, R.M. (1930/2012). *Letters on God and Letters to a Young Woman.* Evanston, Illinois: Northwest University Press.
6 Proust, M. (1871–1922/1982). *Remembrance of Things Past, Vol II.* p. 787. New York: Random House, Vintage Books.
7 Proust, M. (1871–1922/1982). *Remembrance of Things Past, Vol II.* p. 809. New York: Random House, Vintage Books.

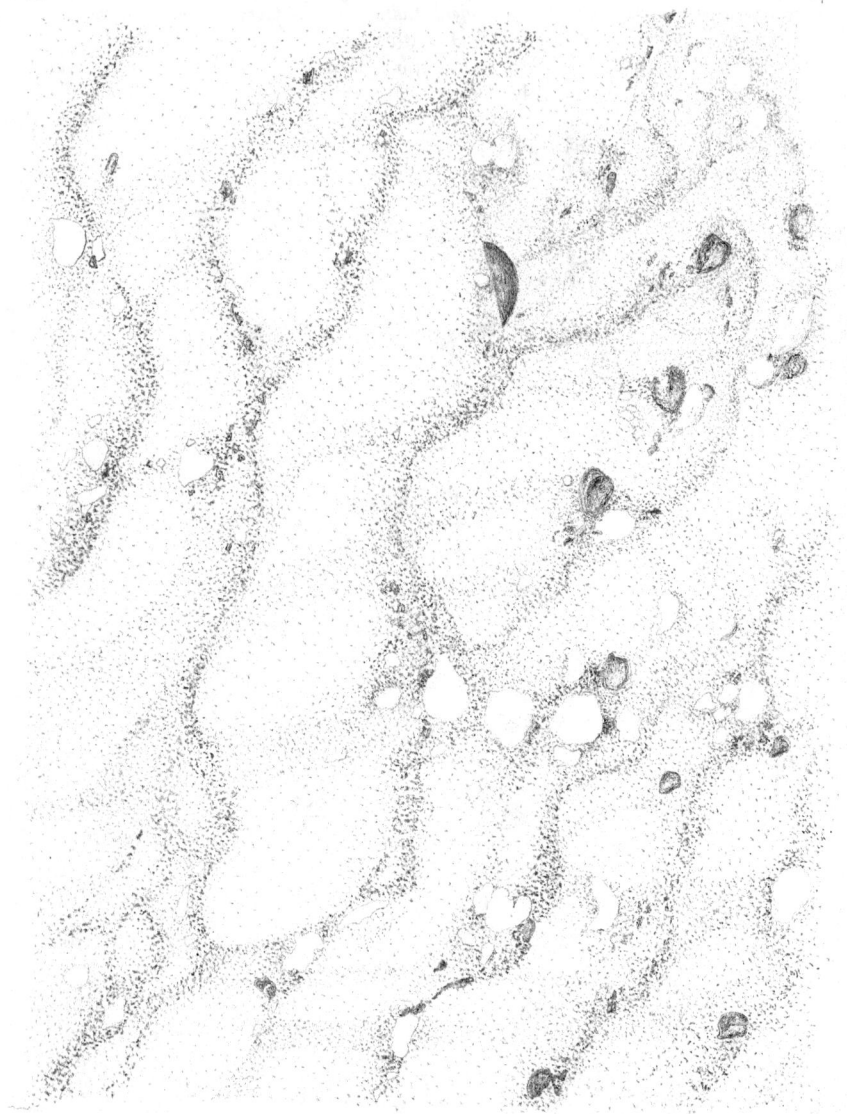

Chapter 2

A disturbance of memory

A yearly recurring event for Freud was a journey to the Mediterranean countries in the company of his younger brother, Alexander. One of these journeys took them, one early autumn, to Trieste, from where they planned to continue south through Italy and further to Corfu. However, an acquaintance warned them against such a voyage, claiming it would be too hot and difficult. Why not use the occasion to visit Athens, he suggested. Athens would offer a far larger and more enriching experience. The helpful and eager man told them how they, the very same day, could embark on their journey by sea.

What was remarkable about this journey that took the two brothers to Athens is linked to a rather peculiar experience Freud had and to the fact that it took him 32 years to describe this experience, despite that he recurrently thought about it, without finding a satisfactory explanation.[1] It was his friend, the writer Romain Rolland's seventieth birthday that gave Freud the occasion to once more reflect on his remarkable experience. Freud had great esteem for Rolland, and the two regularly corresponded between 1923 and 1936, but actually met only once. Rolland was not only a significant writer but had, as Stefan Zweig writes in his book *The World of Yesterday,* an exceptional literary talent besides being a courageous and insistent proponent of world peace. Rolland took great pains to unite the artists and intellectuals of Europe during the First World War. He possessed a humanitarian and moral sensibility combined with great inner freedom, and he was the man, writes Zweig, who at a critical moment in history was to become Europe's conscience.

Freud was intent on expressing his admiration for his friend, and of being equal to Rolland's stance as a humanist and courageous spokesman of truth and righteousness, but had to admit that his ability fell short. He therefore had to content himself with the modest gift of a letter of congratulation, written by "a creature who has seen better days"[2] – a heartful confession from an 80-year-old, which was, however, contradicted by the charming and insightful story he enclosed in the letter. Here we witness a fascinating example of how an apparently mundane event is shown to contain a psychological complexity that only afterthought can grasp and elucidate.

While the two brothers wandered the streets of Trieste, they thought of the suggestion of changing travel plans. Despite the idea of going to Athens being settled, it had placed them in a sad and despondent state of mind. In their minds, they foresaw all the trouble connected with a change of plans, while they – not without a certain displeasure – arranged the trip to Athens.

Let us try putting ourselves in the brothers' place. Since their youth, they had dreamt of travelling, and their interest in history and archaeology had, naturally, made Athens and the Acropolis the aim of their dreams and hopes. And there they stood – close to their goal – and were gripped by despondency. In this mood, they boarded the ship, arrived in Athens, and for the first time stood on the Acropolis, letting their gaze fall on the surrounding landscape. At that moment, Freud had a remarkable notion, which became the pivotal point of the extraordinary experience he chose to describe to Rolland. The notion is as follows: "*So all this really does exist, just as we learnt at school*".[3] Freud italicised the sentence, to underline its power. The notion must have puzzled him, as Freud could not conceive that he at any point in time had doubted the existence of the Acropolis. His puzzlement grew no less as the notion seemed to originate from a different person than the one that was at that moment standing on the Acropolis, observing its surroundings. The absurd thought was accompanied by a particular split in Freud's personality. The person who was thinking the thought seemed to acknowledge a truth that had been previously doubted. With a modicum of exaggeration, writes Freud, one could liken it to a person, wandering the shores of the Loch Ness, suddenly catching a glimpse of the famous monster and exclaiming: "So it really exists". Of course, we have no doubt that the Scottish monster is a fable and not a real phenomenon. The comparison thus serves to illustrate that something in our psyche sometimes intervenes and makes it difficult to maintain normal judgement of reality.

The other person, who registered this doubt of the historical site's existence, was just as surprised. This person was utterly ignorant that the existence of the Acropolis had ever been in doubt.

Let us dwell a moment on Freud's particular notion. It is the kind of idea that arrives spontaneously and comes out of the blue, so to speak. Freud's idea calls for attention if only for its being so different from the experience most people would have, standing for the first time on the Acropolis and viewing its greatness. They would probably acknowledge the experience by exclaiming: "How wonderful, how extraordinary", precisely because it exists there before their eyes. Freud's idea: "So it really exists" expresses doubt of the existence of something real. What is this doubt that can strike us and give us the impression of being split or cleft between a part that experiences and another part that stands outside and askingly observes the experience?

As always, Freud conceives of a number of explanations, which seem immediately plausible, only to later reject them as banal. An immediate explanation lies in the difference between actually experiencing something and having read about it. Freud had previously tried to explain the event on the

Acropolis with the element of surprise inherent in standing before such an important cultural monument as the Parthenon of Athens, which had until then existed for him only in the form of numerous portrayals and descriptions. But he was not at peace with this explanation. More was at stake, and only the fact that he thought about this event so long after its taking place is testimony of it having lived on in him, insisting on being expressed and understood. Another explanation, which he also rejects, could be that he, as a schoolboy, had been convinced of the existence of the Acropolis, but had unconsciously, for some reason or other, refused to believe it. First on seeing it with his own eyes, the conviction had reached his unconscious. An explanation, he adds, that sounds profound, but is hard to prove. We are reminded of the doubtful attempt to drag explanations from the unconscious like rabbits out of a hat.

It was, however, not only the strange notion that demanded an explanation, but also the feeling that had preceded it, when the brothers were gripped by despondency in Trieste at the prospect of changing their travel plans. Freud had no doubt that there must exist a link between their inexplicable oppression and the remarkable thought that struck him.

The despondency could be understood in the light of the well-known expression that something is too good to be true. We have won a million dollars at the lottery, or received a large inheritance, but we can hardly believe it. To give this expression greater depth and weight, Freud refers to his clinical experiences with patients. It is normally the case that people fall ill because of lack and frustrations, but for some it is the opposite. They fall ill when something succeeds, or when long-harboured and powerful wishes have the prospect of coming true. The famous Norwegian author Henrik Ibsen had a keen eye for such characters, who are gripped by terror at the prospect of having their deepest wishes fulfilled.[4] There is something demonic in people who dread the good, as Søren Kierkegaard[5] as well as Freud have remarked, and it could be added that these people not only dread the good, but can find remarkable pleasure in punishing themselves. Something being too good to be true points to the opposition between our wishes and our dreams, on the one hand, and deference to reality on the other, but the statement also seems to contain a reminder of the impossibility of possessing the unequivocally good. Something within us calls for caution when faced with the desire to give in to dreams and longings. This something has, in psychoanalysis, been conceptualised as the superego. This controlling and pleasure-inhibiting aspect of the subject is a consequence of cultural development which demands restraint, and inflicts a lasting sense of discontent, since we direct anger and frustration inwards, towards ourselves. In other words, we equip ourselves with a chronic sense of guilt, which is, to a certain extent, alleviated when we succeed in directing our discontent to the external world, and call it fate.

When Freud suggests that the doubt that gripped him on the Acropolis was a displacement from the past, it should be understood as there being something in the past that sowed doubt about something being real. And since he had to dismiss the idea that the doubt pertained to the existence of the Acropolis, he had to find this doubt elsewhere. He located it, he claims, in the doubt that he would ever succeed in seeing Athens and the Acropolis. Here we approach the kernel of the story, as Freud understood it. To travel the world and see the cities that were the object of such enthusiasm had been completely out of reach. His family did not have the means for anything so extravagant. More importantly, such a venture would have been synonymous with triumphing over his father. Freud's father had neither the means nor the education to imagine such a journey. As an illustration of how serious the son's ambition and awe of his father's authority had been, Freud turns to his brother and repeats the words Napoleon uttered to *his* brother during the coronation in Notre Dame: "What would *Monsieur notre Père* have said to this, if he could have been here today?"[6]

The events can, up to this point, be summarised as follows: The mere idea that they were to see Athens and the Acropolis activated the dread-tinged emotion associated with triumphing over the father. The anxiety and guilt of challenging the father contaminated the experience and disturbed the sense of reality. A repressed wish appeared and temporarily brought destruction to what should have been unequivocal delight. It tells us that Freud, throughout his life, struggled with the Oedipus complex that became the gravitational centre of his theory of the history of our personal lives, and that the Acropolis and its surroundings might have contributed to activate it. It is here tempting to refer to Sophocles' tragedy *Oedipus in Colonus*. Oedipus, after the murder of his father and marriage to his mother, flees Thebe and arrives at the valley of the Erinyes, or goddesses of vengeance, below the Acropolis. After every kind of mishap and tragedy, Oedipus is eventually able to reconcile himself to his fate. The place, in other words, is not without importance in the activation of the emotionally mixed relationship to the father, that Freud summarized in the Oedipus complex and recognised in himself.

Freud's own explanation deserves attention if only because of the thorough exploration of, and wonder at, the manifestation of something that would not immediately let itself be understood. From a seemingly benign episode we are presented with the complexity of the many levels and dimensions of what we call the psyche. We see how memories arise and are temporarily linked to a denial of a piece of reality which is immediately displaced to the past. To this is added a remarkable split of the personality which is accompanied by feelings of unreality. Freud, in his understanding, laid particular weight on that piece of reality that was denied, and displaced to the past, and had apparently no doubt that it was the relationship to the father that could gather all the pieces of the puzzle into a consistent and incontestable explanation. It is difficult to disagree. The story of the event on the Acropolis appears with such authoritative and irrefutable power that the reader can but acknowledge the way in which Freud puts the different pieces together and agree with the explanation that gathers the threads and seems unquestionable. Nevertheless, it seems to me that the event, as well as Freud's explanation, are open to further interpretation.

I therefore want to add some additional aspects to what Freud called a disturbance of memory and to pose the question if Freud's explanation, regardless of being plausible, might have closed the way to memories deeper and more disturbing than the paternal complex that he had probably been aware of, and had probably reconciled himself with, to the extent that it is possible, long before he chose to write on the events on the Acropolis. This demands that I make a detour through the theory of how unconscious memories interfere with present perceptions and can disturb them. I wish to begin by referring to phenomena of a similar character, which can all be summarized under the heading "when something goes wrong with our judgment of reality". That which goes wrong can either be experienced as something foreign with a touch of the uncanny or can manifest itself as a kind of revelation, a moment marked by intense presence, and a lucidity that many artists have known to make use of.

We are familiar with the phenomenon of déjà vu, where we suddenly experience something we seem to have experienced before. To the same group belong other phenomena, such as being in the process of saying something and suddenly feeling insecure whether we have already said it, or we can experience faulty recognition. We seem to recognise something, but on second thought realise that it was just an impression, not a real recognition. The accompanying feeling of unreality is sometimes associated with external reality, sometimes with our own person, but most often the two feelings coexist. These are brief, isolated episodes that are, however, accompanied by temporary displeasure and momentary disorientation.

These experiences can be likened to the dizziness that Kierkegaard spoke of in his essay on anxiety.[7] When we peer into the deep, or into an abyss that threatens to engulf us, we can feel as if we are losing our foothold, since the world as we know it loses its familiarity. We feel as if we succumb with this world and at the same time are separated from it. In short, there is something ambiguous and uncertain about the situation that seems to coincide with an insecurity about our judgement or sense of reality, with consequent disorientation. One explanation of these phenomena might be that some of the boundaries we normally take for granted have been suddenly suspended or blurred. What is in question is the boundary between internal and external, between subject and object and between the familiar and the foreign. These experiences can be disturbing and anxiety provoking, inducing hallucinations, but can also be revelatory and fascinating. But first and foremost, they are strange, alien. They mark us with their strangeness. The strangeness is linked to the temporary loss of the intimacy which we associate with our self-awareness, and for a brief moment, we experience a form of being that goes beyond the feeling of solidity and reliability that we take for granted in the same way as the air we breathe. Such experiences confront us with the fragility of our existence and can create anxiety, but can also be a powerful incitement to creative activity.

These are experiences with a powerful sensory character, which can be almost ecstatic, since we literally step or fall out of ourselves. Romain Rolland introduced Freud to the phenomenon of "oceanic feeling", which Freud, being the rational thinker he was, found too speculative or metaphysical. But he admitted that the young child experiences a state where boundaries are blurred, and that this state never strictly disappears, but can appear when there is an imbalance in the continuum that links the perception of external reality to the perception of the psychic reality of the internal world. In moments such as these, visual impressions can appear with intense clarity, at the same time as seeming not to belong to the experiencing self. They are moments, we might call, using the Greek term, *Epiphanic. Epiphany* was originally the term for the sudden appearance of God. Today we would probably speak of a moment of extraordinary clarity. The Danish painter and sculptor Christian Lemmerz has said about these moments that clichés are washed from the eyes and that we therefore see the things surrounding us with a new lucidity. My idea is that there is a kinship between these epiphanic moments and the more limited and fleeting experiences we all have, and that Freud summarized under the heading of the psychopathology of everyday life.[8]

The Danish poet Søren Ulrik Thomsen has, in his latest book, *En hårnål klemt inde bag panelet*[9] (Translators note: *A hairpin stuck behind the panelling*), described such an experience, which he himself characterises as an epiphanic moment. It could, however, just as well be described as one of everyday life's small parapraxes. The poet, walking along the canal in Copenhagen, is taken aback by some figures, moving with remarkable slowness in the otherwise hectic crowd, and solely the discrepancy between these two speeds, he writes, rendered the usually familiar street scene a dreamlike glimmering and made him doubt, for a few seconds, what he saw. In such a sudden rupture of the habitual we would probably wonderingly ask ourselves whether our senses are deceiving us. The familiar is disturbed by the unknown or strange.

James Joyce is one of the artists who has explicitly used epiphanies as the original material of his writing. In his early writing, he published fragments of observations, which he called epiphanic. To begin with they were small slips of the tongue and other parapraxes by which people revealed precisely the secrets they wished to conceal. In time, these became a mixture of lyrical passages and small dramatic sequences of events. What is interesting in Joyce's epiphanies, seen from a psychoanalytic angle, is the link between the early, spontaneous epiphanies and the meaning they can be seen to have, thematically and stylistically, for his later writing.[10] Joyce in this way confirms the psychoanalytic theory that experiences which have made an impression, and have therefore been inscribed as unconscious memories, are not coincidental, and that the meaning we can extract from them is revealed later, when they, under similar circumstances, are actualised. Marcel Proust, like Joyce, knew that there lay an artistic obligation in seizing such suddenly appearing moments, such as the view of a church tower from different angles, the blossoming of hawthorn, or the taste of ice cream, and to transform these impressions, giving them beautiful poetic form. Also, Rainer Maria Rilke understood to utilise epiphanic moments and recreate them in artistic form. His book *Stories of God*[11] gathers a number of stories, which are all epiphanic in the traditional sense of the word, in that God is present and intervenes in the sorrows and joys of man.

Regardless of whether these epiphanic experiences have a beautiful, but desolate form, as in Rilke, a lively poetic form as in Proust, a simultaneously very concrete and subtle form, as in Joyce, or a day-to-day and recognisable form as in Thomsen, the same phenomenon is in question. The perceived, which normally appears to consciousness as reliable information of the nature of the external world, suddenly receives an actuality and a presence, that we are not used to associate to sensory reality.

I shall try to explain more closely what happens in these moments, where the experience of reality is shaken. These moments are interesting, because they show that our perception of reality is not as solid as we generally assume it to be. *Reality testing* is the psychoanalytic term for the function, that allows us to discern the perceived and sensed, that belongs to the external world, from that which is but a representation, belonging to the internal world. It is important to underline that reality testing does not imply the existence of a standard for what is real as opposed to what is only imagined. Applied to therapy, such a point of view would imply that our task is only to convince the client that this or that they are anxious about does not correspond to reality, but are unrealistic elements, belonging to the subjective world.

Anxiety may, as we know, eat up souls, but anxiety cannot be mastered by confronting a person with the object in the external world, which anxiety has more or less by coincidence inhabited. The source of anxiety is hidden. Anxiety, as opposed to fear, must be understood as a window to the psychic reality of the internal world, that is to say, to those unconscious fantasies which have created the anxiety.[12]

The judgement of reality does not exist at the beginning of life; something must be added for the child to discern that which is but imagined from what also exists as external. That this is no easy task is manifested in those phenomena where something imagined appears with so sensory a character that we experience it as real. The dream is the most illustrative example of a visual experience that is not created by external influence on the sensory apparatus. Dream images are, on the contrary, the result of a complicated process terminating in the activation of the perceptual system from within. We close our eyes and see images, the evidence of which we do not doubt. In other words, we close our eyes and hallucinate. We normally associate hallucination to the psychoses, but the dream shows us that hallucination is a commonly occurring psychic activity. The dream is created from a movement opposite to that of normal perception and has its origin in thoughts and representations, which find their way to the perceptual system. During this process, thoughts and representations are transformed into visual images, and when we, in a waking state, narrate the dream, we additionally order and structure the dream in accordance with the logic and structure of our conscious thinking. There is no difference with respect to our perception of external reality, which is also subjected to the secondary elaboration of rationality, so that its material appears as a coherent whole.

This hallucinatory activity exists from the beginning of life and is the child's first attempt to re-find the experience of satisfaction which it cannot, by its own means, create. Driven by the need for the mother's presence and the acute need for her help, the child creates, according to the psychoanalytic explanation, a hallucinatory image out of the traces of earlier experiences of satisfaction. It is the following disappointment and frustration, as the hallucinated images do not result in the satisfaction of needs, that drive the child to develop the ability to distinguish between what is only an internal representation and what is also found externally. When the child has developed a solid discernment between internal and external, judgement of reality ensures that hallucinatory activity is held back and inhibited. But it can be activated under particular circumstances, as shown above, and lead to a disruption of the balance between perception and representation, resulting in sudden lucidity and intense presence.

There is, however, another dimension in the transition from the merely hallucinated to a dependable sense of reality, which is more disturbing, and gives the experienced phenomena more depth. It is a dimension related to our own existence and which concerns the fact that we are not only originally marked by the loss, that results in the first differentiation between the child and the parents. The child must live through the disillusion related to the shortcoming of hallucinatory wish fulfilment. All this amounts to our predicament as subjects marked by this double loss. We are, fortunately, able to compensate for the loss that the recognition of reality inflicts on us. We establish an area in the psyche, which maintains a refusal of the primacy of reality. This is the area of fantasy, which, as an intermediary zone between the internal and the external offers a space of experience free from the conceptual limitations of conscious thought. For the child, this is a space for play, while adults find equivalent experiences in the areas of culture and aesthetics. Seen this way, hallucination is the earliest form of fantasy and imagination and thus also the first illusory zone of play and creativity.

Something went wrong on the Acropolis – something related to the area of fantasy and imagination. Freud had for many years dreamt of, read and fantasised about Athens and the Acropolis, and even if seeing these glories with his own eyes was enriching, something was lost. The images he had created of the famous place succumbed in front of the Acropolis of reality. Considering the many years that elapsed between the experience on the Acropolis and Freud's analysis of the event, it had probably affected him on a deeper level. In a moment of existential doubt, he was struck by something disturbing, something with a shock-like character, since it opened the path to the original loss, to the crack or rupture, that marks us as human. In such a moment, it is not only our senses that betray us, and we do not know on what to rely on. We are, for a brief moment, shaken in our foundations, as it is said, and experience the fragility of our existence.

I wish to suggest that something more serious was at stake for Freud than his explanation allows us to guess. I have found a reference to what this might have been in a passage in Freud, where he mentions another disturbance of memory, on which, however, he does not comment. At a certain point, Freud turns to his brother and asks if he can remember how they, on their way from school, spoke of travelling the world. Considering the vast difference in age of 10 years or more between the brothers, it is not plausible that such a conversation had taken place. Freud had another, two years younger brother, Julius, who tragically died a couple of months after birth. Such a loss is not only inherently difficult for a child to bear; the child is, additionally, marked by the grief of the parents, which can leave a lasting image of a mother who is inaccessible and lost in her own sorrow. Freud had on several occasions linked the loss of Julius to distinct experiences of anxiety that plagued him later in life, and it might be the memory of Julius that had inserted itself between Freud and his brother Alexander, who accompanied him on the journey to Athens. It is not improbable that the loss of his brother Julius had installed itself into Freud's experience of the Acropolis, and that the doubt he gave expression to went deeper than his own investigation surmises. It was not this landscape of early childhood that Freud was to choose as the frame of his story. If it made itself known in the experience on the Acropolis, it was displaced to a theme with which Freud felt more comfortable, and which could give the story the context and incontestability he aimed at. He ends his letter to Rolland by referring that it was the son's *reverence* for the father that was as stake in his disturbance of memory on the Acropolis.

Freud, unlike the artists here mentioned, had neither the ability nor the inclination to use these temporary lacks and losses in his creative endeavour. He did not create a poetics of the return of the lost in the medium of dreams, hallucinations and fantasy, but created a form of thinking, an afterthought so to say, that occurred after the events that provoked it, and he had the ability, with the power of thought, to summarise the enigmatic and alien, and make it familiar.

Notes

1 Freud, S. (1936). A disturbance of memory on the Acropolis. *The Standard Edition of the Complete Psychological Works,* Vol. XXII, pp. 250–257. London: The Hogarth Press.
2 Freud, S. (1936). A disturbance of memory on the Acropolis. *The Standard Edition of the Complete Psychological Works,* Vol. XXII, p. 239. London: The Hogarth Press.
3 Freud, S. (1936). A disturbance of memory on the Acropolis. *The Standard Edition of the Complete Psychological Works,* Vol. XXII, p. 241. London: The Hogarth Press.

4 Ibsen, H. (1886/1960). *Rosmersholm.* Translation by James McFarlane, Oxford University Press.
5 Kierkegaard, S. (1981). Anxiety about the good. In: *The Concept of Anxiety*, pp. 118–136. Editor Reidar Thomte. Princeton, New Jersey: Princeton University Press.
6 Freud, S. (1936). A disturbance of memory on the Acropolis. *The Standard Edition of the Complete Psychological Works,* Vol. XXII, p. 247. London: The Hogarth Press.
7 Kierkegaard, S. (1981). Anxiety about the good. In: *The Concept of Anxiety*, pp. 118–136. Editor Reidar Thomte. Princeton, New Jersey: Princeton University Press.
8 Freud, S. (1905/1933). The psychopathology of everyday life. *The Standard Edition of the Complete Psychological Works,* Vol VI. London, The Hogarth Press.
9 Thomsen, S.U. (2016). *En hårnål klemt inde bag panelet, s. 66.* København: Gyldendal.
10 Joyce, J. (1916/2008). *A Portrait of the Artist as a Young Man.* Oxford World's Classics. In this powerful autobiographical novel, anxiety and guilt are the central themes and trace a line back to Joyce's epiphanies.
11 Rilke, R.M. (1930/2012). *Letters on God and Letters to a Young Woman.* Evanston, Illinois: Northwest University Press.
12 Gammelgaard, J., & Kristiansen, S. (2017). The screen function of unconscious fantasy. *The Scandinavian Psychoanalytic Review,39*(2):1–11.

Chapter 3

The mystic writing pad

In Sigmund Freud's day, one could, in certain shops, buy a simple writing instrument, constructed in a special way that at the same time as it retained writing, it offered a receptive surface for new inscriptions. This instrument tempted with a kind of magic. It did not look like much, but on closer inspection, revealed a construction which roughly corresponded with the structure and function of the psyche conceptualised by Freud, on which he had speculated for many years. Onto this mystic pad he now projected his entire conceptualisation of the many layers and functions of the psyche.

Freud's text on the mystic writing pad does not look like much, either.[1] It is only six pages long and is just as interesting for what it omits as for what it contains. Central to the text is the relationship between perception of the external world and recollection or remembering, and the essay's primary aim is to visualise an idea which can be traced to his earliest works.

As early as while working on the first draft of the description of the psychical apparatus, as he called it, Freud pointed out that consciousness and remembering are mutually exclusive. Characteristic for consciousness is that the cathexes accompanying sense impressions do not leave lasting traces, but so to speak disappear upon becoming conscious. The condition for something being stored in the psychical apparatus, on the other hand, is a certain form of violent intrusion and a system which is sufficiently cathected with psychic energy to offer resistance.

Remembering is such a system, and remembering, at this point in the development of the theory, could therefore be defined as the ability to allow oneself to be lastingly changed by events that had taken place at some earlier time.[2] Remembering is, in other words, the internal representation of external events, which is to say that remembering is not one of the many functions of the psyche, but its very essence. Freud's point was that nothing, sensed or experienced, disappears, but is stored in a consecutive series of memory systems, as in an inner archive. He had numerous thoughts on how to visualise such an apparatus. One of the more spectacular attempts in this direction is his representation of the psychical apparatus as the city of Rome, with its long history.[3] If we assume that its topography and historical buildings are all preserved, and that we in one glimpse are able to grasp the successive transformations of the city, and transfer this image to the psychic apparatus, it follows that all that has happened to us, and fallen into our system of remembering, will appear before our inner eye. This image, however, is pure and sheer fantasy, as it pushes the boundaries of our capacity for representation to the point of the absurd, writes Freud. But the attempt reveals how far we are from creating a clear depiction and understanding of the peculiarities and variability of psychic life. This, however, did not stop Freud from constructing a number of visions of how the human psyche must be construed in order to perform the functions that we have knowledge of and insight into. The point of departure for the attempt to create a model of the psychic apparatus was, as previously mentioned, the postulate that consciousness and remembering are incompatible within one and the same system. Impressions received from the senses are not retained in those systems that Freud summed up under the one term as the system perception/consciousness, but rather in underlying systems of memory. Even if Freud continued working on the idea of perception/consciousness and memory as two systems with mutually exclusive functions, it was first in connection to the mystic writing pad that he found an instrument which contained a receptive as well as an underlying surface for retention.

The question of how we help ourselves remember was the starting point for the succession of thoughts which unfolded in the essay on the mystic writing pad. Generally, we write down what we wish to remember, and the tools available in Freud's time were the sheet of paper, the slip of paper and the slate. Today we have replaced these simple tools with advanced electronic devices, but the principle is the same. They are materialisations of our memory system. While the computer of our day is equipped with a twofold function, being free to receive new text while simultaneously saving it in an underlying system, all the writing tools available in Freud's time had an inherent limitation. The sheet of paper was rapidly filled and must be replaced with a new one. On the other hand, the sheet of paper retained the writing impressed on it. The slate had an infinite capacity of reception, but could not simultaneously retain what was once written. The mystic writing pad showed itself to achieve more, as it could both offer a constantly receptive surface and hold lasting traces of the inscription, and it was precisely this Freud used as an image of the different and mutually exclusive functions of the psychical apparatus.

The mystic writing pad consisted of a slab framed in paper. The slab was made of wax, and covered by a thin transparent sheet, fastened at the top of the slab but free at the other end. The sheet consisted of two layers, one of celluloid and beneath it a thin sheet of wax paper. The top sheet ensured that the inscription was transferred to the wax slab, and the grooves created by the inscription were manifested as a kind of writing which could be likened to the writing on clay or wax of antiquity, writes Freud. If one wished to erase the writing, it sufficed to lift the double top sheet from the wax slab.

The contact of the double cover sheet and the wax slab, which revealed the inscription, was thus broken and could not be restored when the two surfaces once more touched. The mystic writing pad was now blank and ready to receive new notations, while the grooves in the wax slab remained, almost like invisible and illegible writing.

Naturally, Freud's interest in this mysterious pad did not consist in the technical qualities of this simple writing tool, but in shedding light on how the psychical apparatus must be construed in order to solve the complex task of receiving and also preserving impressions. The double top sheet corresponds to the system of perception and consciousness and the wax mass to the deeper system of memory. The text, however, does not mention the selective effect of the system of memory on such perceptions that are taken up by consciousness, neither does it mention any other characteristics of the two systems. The assumption that perception cannot become conscious without the intervention of memory had proved itself decisive in clinical work, where it was obvious that nothing of what we experience is lost, but is stored in the systems of memory, from where it influences every conscious phenomenon.

Freud was not alone in postulating that perception cannot be reduced to the senses. Contemporary cognitive theorists have argued that information is not a one-way process from the external to the internal, but that the subject in equal measure informs the world, that is to say, shapes it from within. Additionally, French phenomenologist Maurice Merleau-Ponty has, in his essay on perception, written "nothing determines me from the outside", and he continues, "not because nothing acts on me, but, on the contrary, because I am from the start outside myself and open to the world".[4] To my mind, this is one of the most beautiful expressions of the openness and vulnerability that can be deduced from Freud's description of the perceptual system, which is characterised by being open and receptive to new impressions. The perceptual system does not only receive impressions from outside, but can also be activated from within, as illustrated by dreams and hallucinations. There exists a streak of hallucination in perception, or as Merleau-Ponty has written: "Every sensation carries within it the germ of a dream".[5] Had Freud encountered such a formulation, he would have been enthusiastic.

He was probably equally enthusiastic upon finding the simple writing tool which could visualise his conception of the psychical apparatus. The double sheet reminded of the way in which he had described the perceptual system. The systems of perception and consciousness were placed at the outer border, thus constituting the interface of the psychical apparatus and the external world, in line with the idea that the perceptual system receives stimuli from without. The perceptual system, like the writing tool, consists of two layers. On the outside is the so-called stimulus barrier, which protects the underlying perceptual system from excessive stimulation from without, in the same way as the celluloid paper protects the underlying wax paper, which would probably tear, if written upon directly.

In his enthusiasm over the numerous similarities, Freud was less concerned with the differences between the mechanical and the psychical apparatus. I will attempt to follow Freud's text, and point out two problems that are not addressed in his brief, condensed text, but pose open questions. The first problem concerns how the idea of the incompatibility of consciousness and perception could be transposed to, and enrich experiences from, clinical work and everyday life. The second problem concerns the question why Freud chose a writing tool to illustrate the psychical apparatus.

Generally, the mystic writing pad with its two separate systems could illustrate a significant characteristic of the psyche. The human psyche simultaneously contains innumerable layers of translation and displacements of signification *and* the vulnerability and permeability of absolute presence.

The emergence of the conception of the deep structure of the psyche as a layered system of memory traces, between which rewritings and reformulations take place, can be traced as far back as to Freud's work with hysterical patients. The interpretation of unconscious material was thus consequently revealed as an infinite process, terminating at the borders of knowability and interpretation. This border was, in *The Interpretation of Dreams*, denoted as the navel of the dream.[6] It is the space where every interpretation encounters a line drawn by the unknown. It is an axiom of psychoanalysis that the unknown exists at all levels of the psyche. Knowledge of the external world is, in principle, as difficult as knowledge of its internal counterpart, and since memory traces can become conscious in the same way as external impressions, there is always the risk of confusion and distortion of reality. Infinite possibilities of interpretation are also found in art and literature, which are open to myriad interpretations, presenting a polysemy of meanings.

The permeability and vulnerability of the psyche are manifested in various kinds of traumatic experience. For instance, the soldier, returning from the terrors of war, has difficulties in leaving experiences of cruelty and terror behind, as these have broken through the stimulus barrier which normally protects against violent sense stimuli. Or we might think of people who have been the victims of sexual molestation or other forms of violence. Today, we are all reminded of the vulnerability of the psyche when we experience the radical cruelty and evil of terrorism. It was precisely the experience of traumatised soldiers, which led to a theoretical understanding of the character of trauma and to the postulation of a stimulus barrier, which was shown to be of even greater importance to the system of perception than the reception of stimuli per se. The stimulus barrier is equipped with its own reservoir of energy, and its primary function is to protect the psychical apparatus from the destructive influence of too great quanta of energy operating in the external world. At this point, I think not only of violent assaults and other traumas. The increasing flow of information and bombarding of the senses through social media have created other threats and shocks besides "shell shock", which was the starting point for the hypothesis of the stimulus barrier.

Psychic trauma could illustrate what happens in the unconscious when the stimulus barrier is incapacitated, and the boundaries of the psyche broken. Experience from work with traumatised patients has necessitated a differentiation between physical and psychical trauma. When a physical trauma has broken through the stimulus barrier, its further destiny can take two paths. The trauma can find its place in the system of unconscious memories, and like other repressed representations can, under the influence of certain later impressions, return to consciousness – or threaten to. Such a psychical re-traumatisation, experienced by many soldiers, can occur several years after the actual trauma's taking place, and be, if possible, even more unbearable, as it strikes the ego from within, leaving it helpless against catastrophic anxiety and feelings of derealisation. It could also be the case that the trauma leaves nothing behind but an empty space, a form of non-representation of the original shock. The trauma occurred, but found no space in the psyche, leaving a void or emptiness, where a memory trace should have been. It is self-evident that particular resources are necessary in the work with such cases of re-traumatisation. It is of no avail to attempt to bring the original trauma into conscious memory. Therapeutic work in this phase must address the breakdown of the internal world rather than focusing on the external world.

Under normal circumstances, however, there are several factors that protect the system of perception and consciousness from overwhelming impressions. First, external impressions must have a certain structure to be registered by consciousness, and the same applies to internal stimuli. Both kinds of stimuli undergo transformations before reaching consciousness. So-called reality testing consists in the differentiation of what comes from without from what belongs to the representations of the internal world. It is only when a representation of internal origin can be found in the external world that a judgement of reality takes place. Finding an object in the external world is therefore a re-finding. This description of the judgement of reality has an important implication for therapeutic practice. We do not help our patient by claiming that his/her conceptions do not represent the objects of reality. Work must focus on the fantasy world of the patient, and on uncovering the motives and meaning of these conceptions.

Attention is another important and protective function, in that it periodically searches the external world with the aim of securing that its data are familiar, in case a need should arise. Attention, however, also anticipates needs rather than simply waiting for them to arise, and creates "marks" in the experiential world, thus depositing the results of this periodical conscious activity. Linked to attention is the attraction of wishes, exerted by memories tied to situations of gratification, and which, being cathected by great quantities of energy, are capable of becoming conscious. The function of attention and the attraction of wishes operate in the same way, since they are both capable of mobilising perception; the first through an appropriate consideration of the external world, while the second follows the pleasure principle and therefore seeks pleasure-producing objects in the external world. For better or worse, both searching systems are construed to protect from excessive sense stimulation, while simultaneously limiting the subject's "outlook". This limitation is a consequence of protection from excessive stimulation also implying a habituation. The reception of shock is alleviated through the mastery of sense stimulation and the dream as well as memory come to its aid. Remembering helps us by giving us time to organise the reception of stimuli. Habit also helps, as we get used to experiences, which would have had the character of shock without it. Habituation of this sort implies that impressions, which would have belonged to the category of shock or surprise, lose this character. This could be illustrated through the horror stories to which we are exposed through the intrusive sensation hunger of the media, which to some extent make us immune, even in the face of deeply tragical events.

To a lesser extent, shock can be conducive to a widening of the senses and a heightened receptivity to new and surprising impressions. Impressions which, so to speak, trick attention and consciousness, can get direct access to the system of memory, with the effect that memories not directly available to consciousness mingle with new, but similar impressions, which is often experienced as a powerful increase in intensity. Memory traces, created without the intervention of consciousness, are often stronger and more durable, while impressions powerfully cathected by consciousness conversely leave weaker memory traces. The conscious distraction of attention is an artistic means frequently used by writers, and not least by directors of film and theatre, while poets have made use of the ability to capture such deep memory traces which are not detected by the logic of conscious thinking. On the contrary, these lead their secret lives in the midst in scents, colours and other powerful sense impressions, from which they can be retrieved, in the encounter with suddenly arising, similar impressions. Walter Benjamin[7] has introduced the idea of the small shocks of artistic experience, and he has in this context made use of Freud's assumption of the incommensurability of consciousness and remembering and applied the idea to Marcel Proust's voluntary and involuntary memory. Only that which has never been a conscious experience, and which the subject has not registered as an experience, can become part of involuntary memory, and these are the only memories that provide material for the artist. While involuntary memories safe-guard remembering, recollection or voluntary memory attempt to dissolve it.

Freud's model of the psychical apparatus localises Proust's involuntary remembering within a theoretical system, while the poet supplements the theory with experience. Proust writes: "For the truths which the intellect apprehends directly in the world of full and unimpeded light have something less profound, less necessary than those which life communicates to us against our will in an impression which is material because it enters us through the senses but yet has a spiritual meaning which is possible for us to extract".[8]

Only those impressions which, so to speak, sneak past consciousness and are stored in the system of remembering, can endow later, similar impressions a particular quality quite different from the sense impressions captured by consciousness. For many years, the village of Combray, where Proust's protagonist had spent part of his childhood, was barely and scantily remembered, until the taste of a Madeleine cake brought him back to the manifold atmospheres and sense impressions which had been held captive by the limitations of consciousness and recollection. Proust unhesitatingly asserted that the past is to be found in layers which only coincidence allows us to discover. Our conscious memories, or recollections, will never allow us to extract anything besides a weak imitation of an earlier experience, since they are circumscribed by the logic of conscious thought. The question, from this point on, is how and why the poet accesses this internal landscape, exiled by reason, living its secret life in scents, colours and other sense impressions, and how he manages to convey these to the reader. Proust's way was through involuntary memory. For Freud, it was the dream that brought relegated childhood impressions back on the scene of dream life.

The condensed representation of the psychical apparatus with the help of a simple writing tool attempted to unite two opposing functions, a system of perception and a system of consciousness which receive sense impressions, with a system of remembering, which stores these impressions. It is clear that the focus of interest in the mystic writing pad was the perceptual system, but seen from the point of view of inscription. Long before introducing the word system, Freud spoke of types of inscription, and later, in *The Interpretation of Dreams*, he again spoke of inscription, this time of pictorial inscription, on which the dream as well as its interpretation revolved. In the text on the mystic writing pad, it is a matter of a slab, of which the underlying wax mass retains the furrows of what was once a recognisable form of writing, but which dissolved upon lifting the cover from the wax slab.

At this point it would have been but a short step to endow the mystic pad with the magic found in the far more dynamic life of dreams, which demonstrates that when it comes to the psychical apparatus, it is not only a matter of our being written upon. We ourselves write, driven by an instance within us which constantly weighs our perceptions, be they internal or external. This instance cannot be other than the wax slab, or the unconscious memory traces. One of the most fascinating expressions of the emergence of such writing, stemming from memory traces, is the dream, which in its own particular way produces a kind of text, so different from what we usually understand as text, that it is doubtful whether it is at all to be called text. The production of the manifest dream takes place through a complicated process, where impressions from waking life have created a connection to unconscious memory traces beyond conscious attention. From this point on, the dream work consists in the breaking and remaking of the coherent, logical thoughts of waking life and transforming them into dream images, projected onto the internal dream screen. What is in question is thus both a process of dissolution and one of subsequent reshaping of the resulting elements into a completely different form. Dream thoughts are broken up, dissolved and condensed, and the logical bonds joining the thoughts are subjected to the so-called primary process, which reigns in the unconscious and is in many ways different from the secondary process of waking life. The logical laws of thinking do not apply. Here reigns freedom from contradiction, such that opposites and contradictory tendencies exist side by side without cancelling each other. On the contrary, they come together as compromise formations, under the influence of the force through which unconscious wishes force their way to gratification. The dream is simultaneously narrative and gratification. It is both wish and fulfilment of the wish. Neither is there, in the unconscious primary process, anything equivalent to negation. "No" does not exist, and the same applies to the representation of time. To this is added that the representations of the unconscious system of memory are not verbal, but to a different extent consist of sense qualities, with a thing-like character. Neither do they obey conjunctions such as "because", "if" or "either-or", which bind language. The dream must therefore leave the re-establishment of lost coherence to interpretation. The representations of the unconscious are, furthermore, laterally aligned, and can shift places. In other words, the primary process elaborates material in a way that in many respects differs from the secondary process of waking and conscious life. When the result of the primary process' work appears in a dream, there has, however, been a kind of adaptation to secondary process thinking. Consequently, the dream is deployed in a form acceptable to consciousness, as it disposes of certain mediums of expression, among which condensation and displacement are the most important. Condensation consists in several representations being gathered into one, whereby common traits are magnified, while particular traits slip away and become insignificant. Displacement refers to affects, which, not being bound to particular objects, can move from one object to the other, with the result that it is impossible to identify an object through its accompanying affect tonality. Thus, we often carry feelings and moods from dreams into our waking life, without knowing what these moods refer to or where they come from.

In Freud's condensation and displacement mechanisms, linguists have recognised the rhetorical figures of metaphor and metonymy, and suggested that the dream speaks with the speech figures of rhetoric. In Freud's *Interpretation of dreams,* they have, to some extent, found confirmation that the dream can be read as a text of sorts. Freud differentiated between the dream's manifest content and the latent dream thoughts, which he described as "two representations of the same content in two different languages", and while dream thoughts are plainly understandable, as we recognise them from our waking life, the content of the dream is presented in pictorial language, the signs of which must, one by one, be translated into the language of dream thoughts. The pictorial sequences and tableaux of the dream thus should not be regarded as visual images, but read as signs and syllables in need of de-crypting. The dream images are, writes Freud, like the parts of a picture puzzle, and "if we attempted to read these characters according to their pic-torial value instead of according to their symbolic relation, we should clearly be led into error".[9] Regarded as a pictorial composition, the dream becomes absurd and meaningless. Seen as a picture puzzle or rebus, on the other hand, where each picture is to be replaced with a syllable or word, which in one way or other can be symbolised, or illustrated by the picture, the dream emerges as a meaningful statement. To conclude, from a psychoanalytical point of view, the dream is pictographic and not pictorial.

One senses a contradiction in the theory of the dream and of dream work. On the one hand, the primary process refers to the way in which the un-conscious structures psychic material. What is in question is the non-verbal form of thinking – thinking that doesn't know that it thinks. The unconscious contains "thing-presentations" and not "word-presentations", and the syntax and logic of language are absent. On the other hand, the dream makes use of certain stylistic elements, which have been likened to the stylistic figures of rhetoric, and it is claimed that the meaning of the dream is not to be found in in its pictorial composition, but in its pictography. That is to say that the dream can be described as an aspect of thinking and language. The dream is a pic-tograph, a picture puzzle, where images follow each other and are converted into words, which require a context to be deciphered and translated. But is not the dream stripped of its magic, when placed within the boundaries of what can be grasped by thinking and language? Is the dream not primarily a vehicle for moods, and isn't the world of dreams precisely characterised by its pictorial composition? The dream does not think – or at least, it does not know that it thinks. The dream is further characterised by the absence of a subject. Even if we are always present in our dreams, we rarely see ourselves dreaming. We do not exist as subjects in our dreams, but are invisibly present as part of the dream landscape. We often carry the mood in which the dream places us into our waking life, if only as a brief experience in the limbo between dream and wakening, while dream and sleep slowly drift away. At other times, the at-mosphere of the dream inhabits us for several hours, without our being able to link it to any particular events, let alone understand its significance. Freud insufficiently utilised the insights gained from his work on the dream, the joke and the symptom regarding the primary process of the unconscious. On the contrary, he came to insist on what the dream had taught him – that the dream is a different form of thinking, but a thinking far removed from its conscious counterpart. The distortion that takes place during dream work is the result of a psychic functioning, continues Freud, which remains unconscious and makes itself known at night. This must mean that it is not only the work of repression or censorship that distort the dream, but the presence of a completely different mode of functioning of the psychic apparatus, active when "it is freed from inhibition". One could also express this by saying that in dream life we are exempted from the limitations of thinking and language, as well as from considerations of reality. The dream avails of an expressive mode compatible to emotions, moods and passions, a mode which utilises images and pictorial compositions, which should not be understood as other than what they are. They are images of emotions and atmospheres.

It was the observation of the incompatibility between the systems of perception and that of remembering which brought Freud to speculate on how the psychical apparatus must be constituted, in order to ascertain ongoing attention to sense data, and simultaneously comprise a continuously receptive surface. In the mystic writing pad, he saw an illustration of how both functions were encompassed in a simple tool. The psychical apparatus was to exhibit far greater magic than any other mechanical, or for that matter electronical, apparatus to be found in the shops then or now. Granting that the linguists could be right when they maintain that the dream speaks with the tropes and figures of rhetoric, it is important to underline that Freud, with the idea of the primary process of the unconscious, went beyond the rhetorical tradition of which linguists regard him as the heir. The rhetorical figures are elements of style that the dream assumes when, in accordance to secondary process thinking, it manifests itself to conscious thinking. The dream, as we dream it, while sleeping, has a completely different character and might be likened to a collage of atmospheric images.

In the unconscious system of memory, Freud found a form of "thinking" which departed from anything we recognise from the processes of waking life, and for the rest of his life, he remained convinced that psychoanalysis, with its theory of the workings of the unconscious, had created something outstanding.

Notes

1 Freud, S. (1924). Notes on the mystic writing pad. *The Standard Edition of the Psychological Works of Sigmund Freud,* Vol XIX. London: The Hogarth Press.
2 Freud, S. (1895). Project for a scientific psychology. *The Standard Edition of the Complete Psychological Works,* Vol I, p. 299. London: The Hogarth Press.
3 Freud, S. (1930). Civilization and its discontents. *The Standard Edition of the Complete Psychological Works,* Vol XXI. London: The Hogarth Press.
4 Merleau-Ponty, M. (1945/2002): *Phenomenology of Perception,* p. 456. Translated from the French by Colin Smith. London: Routledge.
5 Merleau-Ponty, M. (1945/2002): *Phenomenology of Perception,* p. 215. Translated from the French by Colin Smith. London: Routledge.
6 Freud, S. (1900). The interpretation of dreams. *The Standard Edition of the Psychological Works of Sigmund Freud,* Vol IV. London: The Hogarth Press.

7 Benjamin, W. (1966). Til billedet af Proust. (To the picture of Proust) I: *Fortælleren og andre essays*, s. 69–85. (In: The narrator and other essays). København: Gyldendal.
8 Proust, M. (1871–1922/1982). *Remembrance of Things Past*, Vol III, p. 912. New York: Random House, Vintage Books.
9 Freud, S. (1900). The Interpretation of dreams. *The Standard Edition of the Psychological Works of Sigmund Freud,* Vol IV, p. 277. London: The Hogarth Press.

Chapter 4

They suffer from reminiscences

Marcel Proust's *Remembrance of Things Past* is a homage to the creative and binding power of memory. However, memory is also a source of suffering. The death of the protagonist's beloved, Albertine, leaves him defenceless against pain, as the memories of love and suffering linked to her can no longer be corrected by encounters with the living woman. Jealousy, which should no longer torment him, isn't alleviated by tender feelings, since these are unable to find their object. Albertine has no existence outside of his memory, but the feelings accompanying the memories do not belong to the past and cannot be made past. They are present and alive. Neither will the memories of Albertine be confined to her person. The protagonist's own complex self mingles with his memories of Albertine, doubling his pain. The life he lived with Albertine, oscillating between trust and jealousy, becomes alive and present through fleeting impressions, which bring back memories of his beloved.[1]

With the death of Albertine, Proust's narrator made remembering the very essence of his creative endeavour. While Albertine was alive, the narrator's memories of her were linked to a particular sweetness, as the present conjured images of similar happy moments in the past. Upon her death, the memories were imbued with a different, sorrowful quality. Although the recollections were the same, now they brought only pain. In the face of these memories, he had no recourse but to close his eyes and stuff his ears, only to realise that the memories were not exclusively provoked by sense impressions. His spontaneous stream of thoughts, as well, brought memories, and his suffering was not only linked to the regrets and longings Albertine had inflicted, but to an equal degree to the joys she had given. Therefore, all that remained to do was to forget Albertine. But the protagonist is in no doubt that in order to forget Albertine, he must live through all the feelings linked to her and to his life with her. One by one, he must relive them, but in opposite order of his experiencing of them.

The story of Albertine's death contains and indicates the author's insight that the work of mourning is closely related to what we call the work of remembering. When another being is taken up in us, writes Proust, it must take on the form of time, which means that it appears to us through a row of consecutive moments, and as the memory of a certain moment does not know what is to happen later, memories consist of elevated moments, which resist the binding function of time. That, which was engraved in memory, retains its strength and lives on, along with the person included in it at a certain point in time. In this way, memories of a given person multiply, and the work of mourning consequently consists in renouncing or forgetting not just one, but the myriad shapes the person in question has taken in memory. There is, in other words, a healing aspect to the work of remembering as well as to that of mourning – a point which not only Proust has clarified. It is found in Sigmund Freud, in Virginia Woolf and in Søren Kierkegaard. It is interesting that poets as well as philosophers, from their respective fields of experience, have expressed an idea on memory and mourning which is re-found in psychoanalysis.

Psychoanalysis was born in the attempt to understand the symptoms of hysterical patients. When Freud, in collaboration with his colleague Josef Breuer, presented the results of this work in their common publication of 1895, *Studies on Hysteria*, their laconic conclusion was that these patients suffered from reminiscences.[2] What here was in question was not the form of suffering of which Proust writes, neither was it a question of memories of which the patients could speak, but of unconscious remains of memories which were certainly active, but whose meaning lay concealed in the expression of bodily symptoms. Breuer and Freud learned to read the patient's symptoms as bodily, distorted expressions of painful experiences which had the character of psychic traumas. To their surprise, the two doctors discovered that the traumas in question all belonged to the intimate sphere of sexual experience. The theory of trauma was the key to understanding the formation of the hysterical neuroses. Trauma was, in the initial phase of psychoanalysis, defined as the result of sexual violations or humiliations, which after being repressed from conscious memory were converted into the metaphorical language of the hysterical symptom. The possibility of uncovering the symptom's meaning was shown to depend on the understanding of the way the symptom utilised the metaphors and common sayings of language. One patient suffered from pain in one side of the face as an expression of a blow to the face. Another patient had difficulty walking and a limp in one leg – a metaphorical expression of an unconscious fantasy of having committed a sexual faux pas.

The theory was in its way simple, and the method of treatment equally simple. It was at matter of bringing these traumatic experiences to light, and of abreacting the accompanying feelings. The use of hypnosis gave the whole scenario a mechanical character, and proved difficult to effect as well as rather redundant. Some years later, when hypnosis had been replaced by the psychoanalytic "talking cure", and Freud had learned to maintain a restrained and listening attitude, he realised that his trauma theory had been too simple. The relation between an event and the memory of it was much more complex than he had first presumed. Memories do not exist as a "foreign body" which could be brought back to external events in the form of violations or humiliations.

The word "infiltrate" was introduced to express that something was inscribed in the psyche in a far more extensive and subtle way than the expression "foreign body" indicated. Memories are alive and dynamic. They are subject to constant rewritings and are, now and again, inserted into new contexts under the influence of new events. This means that every memory has already been subjected to transformation. There are, in other words, no original or primal memories, and consequently, memories cannot be regarded as testimonies of factual events. At most, one could speak of the source of a memory, and these are always and already a kind of interpretation or translation. Psychoanalytically speaking, memories must always be differentiated from what we understand as recall.

Another important assumption regarding the concept of memory must be added. Memories always arrive with a delay. Tied to the problematic of memory is a reverse causality, which in psychoanalysis is conceptualised by the term "afterwardness". This refers to the gap between an event and its return as memory, and that events and experiences have "historical effect", wherein traces are manifested far later, when the experience appears as a memory.[3] Despite the concept of afterwardness becoming central in the psychoanalytical theory of the psychology of remembering, it has been elaborated in different ways. Carl Gustav Jung's concept "Zurückphantasieren" has guided the idea that meaning is inserted into past events retroactively, while another conceptualisation reverses the time-line and speaks of something becoming active long after being inscribed in the psyche. My contention, however, is that these two temporalities are not mutually exclusive, rather, they ought to be integrated into a third, composite concept. I shall attempt to illustrate this and have once more chosen to make use of Proust's work on memory, which includes many insightful illustrations of how early impressions live on within the narrator, appearing with a delayed effect which has a violent and dramatic strength. But that is not all. The return of impressions as memories implies that with the help of consciousness, impressions can become experiences, and even if this can entail suffering, it also opens for new insight and new understanding, which in the author's universe constituted the peak of his creative endeavour.

The narrator of Proust's *Remembrance of Things Past* was, at the time when the following story takes place, still a young boy capable of losing himself in sense impressions. One day he found himself in the area of Montjouvain, home of the composer Vinteuil, whose music represented the highest, the sublime, the very image of the work the young hero strove to create.[4] Intoxicated by the sight of a tile roof reflected in water, he had lain down in the shade and fallen asleep. This constitutes the seemingly innocent prelude to the narration of an erotic scene, witnessed by the protagonist upon waking from sleep. Through the window he oversees a scene taking place between Mademoiselle Vinteuil and her lady friend, which ends with the two young women, in a state of wild erotic excitement, spitting on the portrait of the dead father. There are many layers of signification in this scene, which strikes the reader with what Walter Benjamin has called "the small aesthetic shocks"[5] of reading Proust. The reader is as unprepared for the scene as the young narrator, and the reader must, like the narrator, wait for an explanation of the connection between the sublime and the profanation, which is depicted in it. The scene is hidden in a pocket in time, and brought to life far later, when the narrator has become a young man.[6] He is now in a small local train with Albertine and initiates a conversation on Vinteuil, of whom he assumes, with a measure of superiority, that Albertine would know nothing. He is immediately punished for his narcissistic arrogance, as Albertine knows the composer well, particularly his daughter and her friend. This revelation strikes him like a blow, as it momentarily brings back the Montjouvain episode. The reader has previously been thoroughly acquainted with the narrator's insane jealousy regarding what he perceives as Albertine's Gomorrah character. The gesture that was central to the Montjouvain episode had lain dormant within the protagonist's mind and is now presented as an irrefutable truth about the desire of certain women. Proust makes his protagonist notice how the effect of an earlier impression, concealed within him, which is then coincidentally associated with an entirely new impression, announces its appearance with a sudden and violent emotional effect. But that is not all. The author has allowed his protagonist to extract a lived experience from the return of his impression as remembering, in the same way as psychoanalytic therapy attempts to. But Proust goes further than a psychoanalyst. Through his narrator's reflection, he makes the reader aware that the shock caused by Albertine's confession had also transported him into a space to which voluntary memory could never bring him. Proust uses the image of a man who, in a state of shock, makes a leap so high that he finds he has landed in another reality, with a depth of experience only faintly suggested by the original impression. Proust's concept of remembering is the very foundation of the work he created and is insightfully described in this as well in several other episodes. The author has given the concept of remembering a poetic dimension that escaped Freud, perhaps because he never quite differentiated recollection from memory.

The phenomenon of remembering lost part of its attraction for Freud at the point when he realised that memory or recollection is not a reliable testimony of the truth. His patient's stories of early violations were not necessarily reflections of reality but rather the expression of unconscious fantasies and desires. While Freud, in his early work, convincingly wrote, "A psychological theory deserving any consideration must furnish an explanation of 'memory'",[7] the concept of remembering slipped into the background the following years, but never entirely disappeared. It was taken up again in the text *Remembering, Repeating and Working Through*.[8] In the introduction to this text from 1914, Freud summed up the insights on treatment that his work had thus far given him. Phenomena such as screen memories and afterwardness had shown that the conceptualisation of remembering derived from the hypnotic technique, inspiring the likeness to the archaeological excavations of treasures of antiquity, needed to be replaced by a hermeneutic approach. Memories were not immediately reliable, as they demanded a work of interpretation. But that was not all. Freud had made the slightly disappointing observation, that many a patient "does not *remember* anything of what he has forgotten or repressed, but *acts* it out".[9] Instead of speaking of past disappointments and offences, patients acted these out in the transference, as demands towards the analyst, without realising that they in this way insisted on the satisfaction and acknowledgement of unfulfilled needs. Seen in the light of blind repetition, it is understandable that Freud firmly insisted that it was a victory for therapeutic work whenever it was possible to lead repetition into the work of remembering.

As the title of the previously cited text suggests, what is in question is remembering as well as working through, but there is nothing to suggest that the two concepts were understood as identical or connected. Working through refers mainly to the phenomenon of resistance and indicates the inherent slowness of psychoanalytic therapy. Interpretation is not enough, and insight is not an instant recognition, but the result of a slow acquisition of lived experience. I would like to postulate that working through and remembering are intimately linked. They are two sides of the same thing and form a united front against repetition. I will develop this in the following.

In contrast to hypnotic therapy, with its focus on discrete memories, the concept of working through suggests that it is the personality as a whole which participates in the work. Seen in this light, working through appears as a process that opposes the character of repetition inherent to unconscious formations by bringing these into harmony with the patient's whole personality. The concept of remembering, which is only suggested in this text, can be fruitfully linked to what Freud says in his later text on mourning and melancholia. Paul Ricoeur[10] has in his work *Memory, History, Forgetting* underlined that as remembering stands in opposition to repetition in Freud's 1914 text, mourning is contrasted to melancholia in the later text. While remembering and mourning precisely represent work, repetition and melancholia can be understood as a kind of short-circuiting of the psychical apparatus. The work effected by mourning consists in a gradual and painful withdrawal of the libidinal energy invested in the loved and lost object. When this work is completed, the ego is again free and able to invest its libido in a new object. It is not far-fetched to think that this work of mourning is effected by a process of remembering, and that the liberating effect of mourning relies on the remembering inherent to it.

There are costs as well as rewards in the work of remembering and mourning, writes Ricoeur. The work of mourning is the price to be paid for remembering, while also being the reward that the work of mourning achieves. The work of mourning is not unlike the patience required of psychoanalysis in attempting to bring repetition under the domain of remembering, as Freud wrote in the article of 1914. Remembering requires not only time, but time to mourn – a statement that contains the essence of the psychoanalytic technique, which strives for a certain abstinence and resignation as a prerequisite for reconciliation with lost objects. Ricoeur proposes that melancholia, freed from the narrow definitions of psychiatry, contains a depth of emotion that can also be found in music and poetry. In reference, among other things, to Beethoven's late quartets and sonatas, he introduces the term "sublime sadness" and claims that mourning, through the dimension of remembering, contains the possibility to transform mourning to something which could be called "sorrowful joy", and since mourning is a necessary aspect of remembering, the same sorrowful joy could crown the work of remembering, as when a poetic image completes the work of mourning.

Virginia Woolf's posthumously published collection of autobiographical pieces, *Moments of Being,*[11] could illustrate Ricoeur's point on remembering and mourning as two sides of the same thing. In her writing, Woolf found the means to work through a loss that had for many years remained unresolved and had prevented a separation from her mother, whom she lost as a young girl. The point of departure for her reflections on remembering was a particular observation linked to occasional experiences which had made a deep and emotionally powerful impression on her. It was not the experiences as such, that were important, but rather the state each of them brought about. She was driven to return to these experiences in memory, to find an explanation to why some experiences brought her to a state of despair, while others left her with a feeling of happiness and contentment. She understood that when she was able to explain the feeling attached to a particular experience, she was no longer passively subjected to it and could embrace it with joy and satisfaction. With the help of language, she could put words to her feelings. Also, she learned that her receptivity and vulnerability to excessively disturbing or frightening experiences implied a wish to understand, and that in her case, understanding came through language. Disregarding the content of such unusual moments, what they had in common was "a peculiar horror and a physical collapse".[12] When she could describe these frightening experiences in words, they became whole and no longer hurt her, and she understood that the great joy and freedom of writing precisely consisted in her putting things together and finding out "what belongs to what". Only when she found this connection could she create what she called "making a scene come right". Memories of her mother and grief over her death, however, never became whole. Neither through remembering and mourning, nor through writing could she get hold of her fears and breakdowns.

Virginia Woolf lost her mother when she was thirteen, and she explains that she, until she was in her forties and had written the captivating novel *To the Lighthouse,* "the presence of her mother obsessed her". She was unable to create a distance to her mother and enclose her in the dimension of remembering. Upon completing *To the Lighthouse*, her obsession with her mother had diminished; she no longer heard her voice or saw her before her. Woolf reflects that, through writing this novel, she had procured what the psychoanalyst offers his/her analysand. She had expressed and thereby explained a deeply felt emotion, but the way in which this feeling was explained through writing the novel was not clear to her. She must instead search for the explanation in later experiences of loss, which on the one hand helped her remember and work through the death of her mother, and on the other hand gave the impetus to inscribe the experience in the form of a novel, thereby freeing herself from the obsession with her mother.

A couple of years after the mother's death, the family was once more struck by a tragic loss, the death of the half-sister, Stella. Woolf was a child at the death of her mother and therefore unable to fathom the loss, look it in the eye and carry it. Stella's death "fell on another substance; a mind stuff and being stuff",[13] which had the openness and anxious receptivity that characterise a fifteen-year-old. It was first upon her sister's death that she could give in to the feelings which, at the time of her mother's death, had been too chaotic and catastrophic to contain, and that she, through an intellectual denial of death, had tried to refute. Later she would think of Stella, and with a phrasing that could have been created by Proust, she realised that the past returns, "for the present when backed by the past is a thousand times deeper than the present when it presses so close that you can feel nothing else".[14] Such moments, her argument continues, were the happiest, not because she was thinking of the past, but because she lived in the present, which was lit from below by the past. In other words, it is in the peaceful moments, where the mind is in balance, that we can embrace the past and make it a part of the present. But, as Woolf's narrative reveals, joy and peace are preceded by a long and painful work of remembering and mourning. Later, she adds, in the spirit of Proust, that "we are sealed vessels afloat upon what it is convenient to call reality; at some moments, without a reason, without an effort, the sealing matter cracks; in floods reality".[15] The reality of which Woolf speaks has scenic character; in other words, it possesses structure and is thereby radically unlike what our recall might present us with. In her novel *To the Lighthouse,* Woolf has created a fullness she was unable to create immediately following her mother's death and has drawn an unusually gripping and complex memory-image of her mother. Unbeknownst to herself, she thereby concluded the work remembering and mourning, made possible only with the help of poetry.

Virginia Woolf's considerations on the release from mourning made possible by poetry are also found in Kierkegaard, who made a couple of his pseudonyms reflect on memory, forgetting and remembering. In *Stages on Life's Way*, Søren Kierkegaard lets William Afham utter the following observations on recall and remembering. Recall is photographic memory. It is particular and limited and is therefore quite different from remembering. "One can remember very well every single detail of an event without thereby recollecting it", writes William Afham in the introduction to *Stages on Life's Way*.[16] Remembering is less precise; it is not focused on particularities, but strives to encompass the whole, strives towards what is essential, and is determined not only by itself, but by its relationship to the ongoing present. What is remembered cannot be forgotten, and if one attempts to throw it away, it returns, "just like Thor's hammer".[17] Remembering is an art, and to master this art, sensitivity to "contrasting moods, situations and surroundings"[18] is required. Remembering is the "ideality" that secures man's continuity in being and makes his earthly existence *uno tenore*, one breath. Attempting to run to the assistance of remembering, continues Afham, "... would only miscarry and punish [me] with the aftertaste of mimicry".[19] Remembering is best achieved through contradictions, writes Kierkegaard, thus preceding Virginia Woolf's observation. If an experience has been exalted, it is best remembered in stillness and solitude. This point is also found in Proust, when he lets his narrator describe how the joy of seeing his beloved's face is but a negative to be developed later, at home, in the darkroom of his mind.[20]

That remembering and forgetting are not opposed is a point made by yet another pseudonym, Aesthete A, in *Either/Or*. Aesthete A praises forgetting as an art to be pursued consciously and methodically. Forgetting is a pair of scissors, we read, "with which one snips away what cannot be used, but please note, under the maximal supervision of recollection".[21] Remembering and forgetting are identical, he claims, and constitute the artistic Archimedean point which lifts the whole world. If forgetting is to be daemonic and effective, something must be placed instead of that which is forgotten, and that is the purpose of remembering. Remembering is according to this philosophical wisdom poetic remembrance. "The more poetically one remembers, the more easily one forgets, for to remember poetically is actually only an expression of forgetting"[22] – an idea almost identical to that expressed in Virginia Woolf's memoirs.

With these scattered observations on the poetic dimension of remembering, Kierkegaard has illustrated the creative aspect of what psychoanalysis terms the work of memory, which, seen in this light, is revealed as the other side of working through. The poets and philosophers thus add a poetic dimension to the work of mourning and remembering of psychoanalysis. Where psychoanalytic therapy consists in reconciliation with original loss as well as inevitable later losses, and is an epitaph over what is forever lost, Proust's *Remembrance of Things Past* forms a cathedral of remembering, which despite the resistance of habit and tedium, is the only way of bringing lost time back. From the depth of these memories, Proust has created a world in which impressions from different points in time are brought together in images which transcend time, and by being thus positioned outside time, add to them a glimpse of eternity. This is not a harmless game Proust finds in the bottom of a cup of tea, but a painful memory, which is shown, not least, by the main theme, which is introduced and repeated only to find its resolution and closure in the last part of the novel, *Time Regained*. Before the narration of the Madeleine cake dipped in linden tea, we have been acquainted with the little boy the protagonist once was, who could not fall asleep without his mother's good night kiss, and the whole story is framed by the events of the fateful night, when the boy's desire to have his mother to himself was fulfilled. The night when the boy's father, for unclear reasons, encouraged the mother to remain with her son; she read to him from George Sand's *François le Champi*, which contains an Oedipal theme with a relevance to the protagonist's later fate that is revealed at a later point in the novel.

In the first part of the novel is an image of the original trauma, which returns when the protagonist, many years later, through a lucky coincidence, reaches for George Sand's *François le Champi*. Here is a both lively and insightful description of how a painful experience is written into the psyche like a fixated or frozen image, which can only much later be brought out of this state, expressed and translated, through the narrator's fable. For a long time, writes the protagonist, while he lay awake at night and tried to think back of his childhood vacations in Combray, he saw only a lit surface, which stood in sharp contrast to a dark background. In the distance he could glimpse the garden path announcing the arrival of Swann, which meant that the mother, on such an evening, would not come to wish him good night. From the garden path, he could see the other rooms and the long stair-case leading to the top of the house, where his own room was. This was where his "undressing drama" took place, and where the mother, on the nights Swann did not visit, would appear – always at the same time. It was, he ends, as if Combray only consisted of the two highest stories of the house, and as if time stood still at seven o'clock. Everything else was dead to him, until the day his mother offered him a cup of tea and a Madeleine cake. Through this image, which is almost like a flashback in visual perspective, Proust has depicted the way in which a traumatic experience is retained as a living memory-image.

It is, however, at a later point, in the palace of Guermantes, that the memory of the strangest and saddest night of his life reappears, and it is the sound of the little bell, which used to announce the arrival of Swann, that brings the memory back. He heard the little bell resound in his mind and was now convinced that to hear the bell clearly, he must dive into himself and find it there, where it went on living. He ends: "This notion of time embodied, of years past but not separated from us, it was now my intention to emphasise as strongly as possible in my work".[23] This idea of embodied time is the entire foundation of Proust's work, and the aforementioned lines testify that this is not an idea created by the intellect, but through lived experience. What now happens is that the narrator interrupts his line of reasoning and entrusts the protagonist to recount the long past experience, which was associated to the tinkling of the little bell. Remembering the evenings when his mother was prevented from giving him the only thing that could calm him, is but one of the memories which, even if bringing great joy, also contained sorrow and despair. As the human body contains past moments with their joys and desires, it can also bring so much pain to the one who loves this body, that he can be brought to wish its destruction. The body, in which time has fastened every memory, can therefore become the eternal and invincible reminder of the suffering which the beloved's body has inflicted on the jealous lover.

There is an obvious leap in the story at the exact point where the narrator is replaced by the subjective rendering of the protagonist, corresponding to the replacement of philosophical observations on embodied time by the painful jealousy of the protagonist, a jealousy which has bound him to his beloved Albertine, and goes on binding him, although she is no longer alive. The protagonist reminds the narrator as well as the reader of how deeply anchored memories of the lost and beloved objects are in the body. Proust's novel contains three voices. The protagonist, who tells the story from the subjective perspective of experience; the narrator, who lifts experiences to a reflecting level; and the author, who orders the material, so that the reader in himself can recognise the way in which discrete events are woven into the protagonist's life and become lived experiences. It is gripping to read how the author has distributed these roles in such a way that it is the protagonist who speaks when concrete events and related emotions are described, while the narrator lifts the impression to a plane where it can be incorporated into a wider context and become experience, as in a successful psychoanalysis.

Proust's work can be read in many ways, but there is no doubt that it is a work of remembering. *Remembrance of Things Past* is a work on the sorrows and joys of wholly concrete remembering, of which the protagonist tells, but it is also a work on the phenomenon of remembering, analysed in detail, and elevated to a reflecting form of poetry, which is at once humane and deeply thought.

Notes

1 Proust, M. (1871–1922/1982). *Remembrance of Things Past,* Vol III. New York: Random House, Vintage Books.
2 Freud, S., & Breuer, J. (1895). Studies on Hysteria. *The Standard Edition of the Complete Psychological Works,* Vol II, pp. 1–253. London: The Hogarth Press.
3 "Historical effect" is a central concept in the theory of history of Hans-Georg Gadamer. I have permitted myself to transfer it to individual history, see Gadamer, H.-G. (1960–1990/2007). *Sandhed og metode.* Aarhus: Academica.
4 Proust, M. (1871–1922/1982). *Remembrance of Things Past,* Vol I. New York: Random House, Vintage Books.
5 Benjamin, W. (1996). Til billedet af Proust. (to the image of Proust) I: *Fortælleren og andre essays,* s. 69–85. (The narrator and other essays). København, Copenagen: Gyldendal.
6 Proust, M. (1871–1922/1982). *Remembrance of Things Past,* Vol I. New York: Random House, Vintage Books.

7 Freud, S. (1895). Project for a scientific psychology. *The Standard Edition of the Complete Psychological Works,* Vol I, p. 299. London: The Hogarth Press.
8 Freud, S. (1914). Remembering, repeating and working through. *The Standard Edition of the Complete Psychological Works,* Vol XII. London: The Hogarth Press.
9 Freud, S. (1914). Remembering, repeating and working through. *The Standard Edition of the Complete Psychological Works,* Vol XII, p. 150. London: The Hogarth Press.
10 Ricoeur, P. (2006). *Memory, History, Forgetting.* Chicago: The University of Chicago Press.
11 Woolf, V. (1976/2002). *Moments of Being.* London, Pimlico, Random House.
12 Woolf, V. (1976/2002). *Moments of Being,* p. 85. London, Pimlico, Random House.
13 Woolf, V. (1976/2002). *Moments of Being,* p. 130. London, Pimlico, Random House.
14 Woolf, V. (1976/2002). *Moments of Being,* p. 108. London, Pimlico, Random House.
15 Woolf, V. (1976/2002). *Moments of Being,* p. 145. London, Pimlico, Random House.
16 Kierkegaard, S. (1845/1988). *Stages on Life's Way,* p. 9. Translated by H.V. Hong & E.H. Hong. Princeton, New Jersey: Princeton University Press.
17 Kierkegaard, S. (1845/1988). *Stages on Life's Way,* p. 12. Translated by H.V. Hong & E.H. Hong. Princeton, New Jersey: Princeton University Press.
18 Kierkegaard, S. (1845/1988). *Stages on Life's Way,* p. 13. Translated by H.V. Hong & E.H. Hong. Princeton, New Jersey: Princeton University Press.
19 Kierkegaard, S. (1845/1988). *Stages on Life's Way,* pp. 13–14. Translated by H.V. Hong & E.H. Hong. Princeton, New Jersey: Princeton University Press.
20 Proust, M. (1871–1922/1982). *Remembrance of Things Past,* Vol I. New York: Random House, Vintage Books.
21 Kierkegaard, S. (1834/1987). *Either/Or,* p. 295. Translated by H.V. Hong & E.H. Hong. Princeton, New Jersey: Princeton University Press.
22 Kierkegaard, S. (1834/1987). *Either/Or,* p. 293. Translated by H.V. Hong & E.H. Hong. Princeton, New Jersey: Princeton University Press.
23 Proust, M. (1871–1922/1982). *Remembrance of Things Past,* Vol III, p. 1105. New York: Random House, Vintage Books.

Chapter 5

Narcissism

"Narcissism" refers to the subject taking him- or herself as an object of love, or more precisely, identifying with the idealised image of him- or herself. The term points to the general situation that we humans simultaneously create an image of ourselves, and paint and value this image in relation to the values and ideals we have assimilated. In other words, it is the self's relation to itself which is here referred to, and this relationship is primarily created in a mirroring or imaginary dimension, which takes place on the individual as well as on the social level. It is through the other, or others, that we become capable of seeing ourselves in the same way as we look at another. Etymologically, the word *narcissism* springs from the myth of the youth who fell in love with his own reflection, and it is precisely the imaginary, or mirroring dimension, that has made the myth pertinent as the frame story for the phenomenon and concept of narcissism. I wish to open my exploration of narcissism with a reference to the Greek mythological character.

Ovid's retelling of the Narcissus myth depicts the despair of being captive to one's own irresistible beauty. Narcissus is enchanted by his own reflection, but at first does not understand what he sees. He sees, but is unable to grasp what it is he sees. Painfully, the truth dawns on him: "This I in thee − I love myself − the flame arises in my breast and burns my heart − what should I do? Shall I at once implore? Or should I linger till my love is sought? What is it I implore? The thing that I desire is mine − abundance makes me poor. Oh, I am tortured by a strange desire unknown to me before, for I would fain put off this mortal form; which only means I wish the object of my love away".[1]

It is a simultaneously beautiful and sad allegory of the imaginary character of narcissism and of the loneliness experienced when a human being is unable to reach out to another. In his exploration of the phenomenon and concept of narcissism, Freud writes that one must love in order not to fall ill, and that one falls ill when one, because of frustration, renounces love.[2] Soren Kierkegaard's essay *The Sickness Unto Death*[3] is one of the most insightful descriptions of narcissistic despair. One can desperately wish to be oneself, which means, precisely, that one is not oneself, or one can desperately wish *not* to be oneself. Disregarding the content of the despair, the result is the same. The subject sinks into a state of desolate isolation. As the myth illustrates, this isolation can have fatal consequences. Narcissus fell ill and died, thereby reminding us that there exists a self-destructive aspect in the mirroring love of self, or as Kierkegaard poignantly has written: Narcissism is a sickness unto death. In the myth, Narcissus became one with his reflection. He died, but left a lasting memento in the form of the beautiful flower that carries his name.

Ovid located the story of Narcissus within the realm of sexuality and love. Linked to the mythical story of the youth who only loved himself is the story of Echo, who had always had a "silly tongue", and when caught by Juno in the arms of Jupiter was, in punishment, bereaved of that which characterised her, thus losing her capacity for independent speech. Hereafter, Echo could only repeat the last word she heard. To this fate was added the misfortune of her falling in love with Narcissus, who loved only the being he found in his reflection.

The couple of Narcissus and Echo became the symbol of impossible love, but also of every lover's mistake. We mirror ourselves in each other and strive to make our beloved see us as the image of the one we would like to be. We love the one who reflects us in accordance with the image, which in technical terms is called the "ego ideal", another word for narcissism. However, the story of Narcissus, gazing at his reflection in the lake, goes beyond the theme of love and points to a crucial condition within what we call the self, or identity. In order to create an image of ourselves, we need to see ourselves from the outside, from another place, which could be the mirror, but just as well another person. Being oneself thus involves a quantum of alienation, in the sense that we can observe and judge ourselves as if we were another. Not only can we look critically upon ourselves, but we can also surpass ourselves and love ourselves, not because we are better than others, but because we feel better than ourselves.[4]

To a great extent, French psychoanalyst Jacques Lacan is to be credited for pointing out the imaginary dimension of narcissism and of the self, as well as the importance of the other in the emergence of narcissism and of the self. With his mirror metaphor, Lacan inscribed himself into a philosophical tradition that insisted that the self is not just *there*, but is created and must be understood as a relation, and not as an entity. I will explore this more closely, when I introduce Lacan's concept of the mirror stage.

In contemporary society, it is not difficult to perceive the mirroring function and its significance for our self-esteem. The most obvious example of the need for mirroring self-affirmation is the "selfie" phenomenon. We take pictures of ourselves in order to view ourselves, often in the company of other selected persons, who thus contribute to increase our self-worth. Reading the myth of Narcissus in the light of the mirroring function, we can interpret the youth's suffering as an expression of his inability to see himself from the outside, and as he has refrained from using the other's gaze on himself, he directs his desire towards an illusory image of perfection. It is therefore not because of his love for himself that Narcissus falls ill and dies, but because he is unable to free himself from the constraint of his idealised self-image.

In the psychological literature, interest in narcissism has focused on people with disturbances in the narcissistic equilibrium, which implies that they oscillate between omnipotent conceptions of themselves and deep insecurity. Being together with these people can be difficult. They often evoke strong feelings of powerlessness and irritation, since they do not allow others to be the object of their love, but in them seek the worth and meaning that they find it difficult to give themselves. In the same way that Narcissus ignored Echo, one can, in the company of a narcissistically disturbed person, easily come to feel ignored and lacking significance. It is, however, important to underline that beyond the self-sufficient surface exists significant suffering. People suffering from narcissistic disorders are lonely people, who instead of a robust sense of self are joyless in relation to themselves. They lack the protective barrier which makes it possible, for most people, to accept adversity and criticism without serious consequences to their self-esteem. Paradoxically, these narcissists function well in social life, provided they are met with appreciation and affirmation. They are remarkably charming and graceful, and thereby confirm that narcissism can be very attractive to others. Echo's infatuation with the beautiful youth never waned, although he repeatedly rejected her. Even in the underworld she remained faithful to her beloved.

However, narcissism is first and foremost a normal and important aspect of self-esteem in general, and the basis of the joy and pride linked to being the one we are, and to what we accomplish. Narcissism is, in other words, intimately bound to the self, or ego.

In psychoanalysis, the ego is different from what we understand as the individual, or the subject as a whole. It is an internal object cathected with libidinal energy, but also an object capable of action. The fact that the ego is libidinally or narcissistically cathected has positive as well as negative implications. Narcissism is the source of joy connected to self-esteem; it is an aspect of play, creativity and love-making, and the seed of those moments of great happiness due to simply being oneself. Narcissism also implies vulnerability in the sense that others, the world and reality are in principle potential enemies, as they can threaten the core of the ego and the subject's identity. Faced with the threats to self-esteem that come from the external world and from other people, the self can be defeated. We are thus hurt by criticism, we suffer adversity, and our person is attacked. The reactions to criticism and to what are felt as attacks on self-esteem are typical narcissistic offences that can, in the worst case, take the form of narcissistic rage, and in pathological cases, and particularly in collective form, become murderous. It is not difficult to catch sight of the importance of narcissism and prestige in conflicts on the individual as well as the social or societal level. It is narcissism, or self-esteem, that leads to the most irreconcilable insults and struggles, where people fight their private fights for the right to be right. Offended self-esteem can from this point release narcissistic rage, which in serious cases can entail psychological as well as physical violence. When we, in the media, read of a man having murdered his ex-lover or wife and the children they had in common, it is rarely a question of jealousy, but rather an expression of narcissistic offence and rage.

Such tragical stories cannot be understood without insight into the psychology of shame. Shame is the dark side of narcissism, while pride is its opposite and constitutes its positive side. It should, however, be mentioned that pride in certain instances serves as a defence against underlying shame. The feeling of shame is linked to the very fact that the self primarily comes into being in a mirroring function, and is intimately linked to social life. Even if we can feel shame when alone with ourselves, it is a consequence seeing and judging ourselves through the other's eyes. It is a feeling with deep psychical roots, and it can activate the most powerful feelings of offence, hurt self-esteem and in the most serious cases feelings of worthlessness.

After these descriptions of normal and pathological narcissism, let us turn to Freud's text.

Freud wrote his essay on narcissism during a visit to Rome in 1914. It is not without importance that it came into being hurriedly, which expressed that the subject powerfully preoccupied him. Just as with his essay on the uncanny in Chapter 10 in this book, there is something incomplete about this text. It is as if Freud is searching for something which is yet unclear, as if he is ahead of the object of his exploration. The text, pointing in different directions without converging into a whole, gives the impression of an experiment of thought not yet ripe enough to be brought to conclusion. The essay on narcissism was to become a terminological parenthesis in Freud's oeuvre, a temporary station before the comprehensive theoretical reworking that followed his introduction of the concepts of ego, id and superego, and not least, the concept of the death drive.

Seen in the light of later works, it is clear that Freud's 1914 text presaged the breakthrough of the theory of the subject, which implied that Freud was obliged to abandon his first drive theory, based on an opposition between ego-drives and sexual drives. The finding that the ego is itself the object of libidinal cathexis, and a reservoir of libidinal energy, meant that the ego-drives and sexual drives could no longer be regarded as antagonistic forces. Freud took the consequence of this insight and gathered the two drives under the term "Eros", which was from this point regarded as the opposite of the death drive. The further study of narcissism was seen to include phenomena as disparate as the perversions, psychoses and love, to mention but a few of the subjects encompassed by psychoanalytical theory.

Some years after the publication of the mainly theoretical essay on narcissism in 1914, Freud had the occasion to delve more closely into the phenomenon. It was the riddle of homosexual object choice that led Freud onto the tracks of narcissism. In his study of Leonardo da Vinci[5], Freud introduced the assumption of a narcissistic stage in the development of the libido, linked to homosexual object choice. It was the mother's all-encompassing love for the boy which brought the young Leonardo to direct his love towards young men, in the same way as he once was loved by his mother. In other words, Leonardo chose objects that reflected the mother's adored boy of early childhood, putting himself in the place of the lover; the position the mother had held in relation to her son. The homosexual choice of object thus reveals a mirroring effect far more complex than the one depicted in the myth of Narcissus. It is to be noted that narcissistic object choice is not limited to narcissism. It is far more common and is an aspect of every love relation.

A year after the publication of the analysis of Leonardo, Freud published his analysis of Senate president Schreber's memoirs.[6] Daniel Paul Schreber was a prominent lawyer and judge, and the memoir of his life and psychotic break-down was read with great interest by influential psychiatrists of his time. The analysis of the Senate president's psychotic break-down allowed Freud to add another dimension to narcissism. As opposed to Leonardo, Schreber was psychotic, and his narcissism took the form of delusions. The break-down in the Senate president's life entailed a loss of the relationship to the world and its objects, following which he attempted to reconstruct himself through grandiose ideas of the universe and himself. In the psychotic break-down, libido is withdrawn from objects in the external world and is directed towards the ego, which thus takes on megalomaniac dimensions. Psychosis is interesting in the study of narcissism, as it illustrates how the gaze of the other, which we do not normally see, but nevertheless feel observed by, can be experienced with a character of reality when it takes the form of frightening paranoid delusions.

Even if the texts on Leonardo and Schreber are based on literary and biographical studies, they serve as illustrations of the role played by narcissism in phenomena as different as homosexuality and psychosis. Also, hypochondria and the general anxiety linked to the fear of being struck by illness illustrate the withdrawal of libido into the ego, whereupon the subject "so long as he suffers, [he] ceases to love".[7] In the aforementioned examples it is a question of libido being withdrawn from the object and invested in the ego, but with different outcomes. Leonardo loved himself in the young men he fell in love with. In Schreber's paranoid psychosis, however, libido was retained in the ego, where it took the form of megalomaniac delusions. On the basis of these two studies, Freud was able to define narcissism as the withdrawal of libidinal energy from objects in the external world into the ego, and in light of this, it became possible to gather a number of disparate phenomena and regard them from the angle of narcissism. There is an implicit limitation in Freud's viewpoint, namely, that it did not in a satisfactory way answer the question of the formation of the ego, which entailed that the ego appeared as an entity closed on itself. Nevertheless, Freud contributed new viewpoints on the ego and on love life, which were the two paths he pursued in his essay on narcissism.

There are two ways in which we choose our love objects, writes Freud. We can choose out of a desire for attachment, which implies that we search for a person who can give us security and caring, or our choice can be determined by a desire for likeness. We choose a person who resembles us in one or several respects. In other words, we choose our love object on a narcissistic basis.

In the first mentioned choice, it is a matter of choosing a love object in accordance with the image originally created by the ego-drives. What one chooses in the other is a displaced image of the primordial, caring and nurturing parent. At this point, there is no opposition between the ego-drives and the sexual drives. The sexual drives lean on the ego drives and take the object of the ego-drives as their model. Following the child's development, this relation is reversed, with the effect that the sexual drives come to support the ego-drives.

It is through the love of the nurturing parents that the child later becomes capable of transferring this love onto itself. The sexual drives and ego-drives from this point operate jointly and have a common aim. We see an example of this when parents coax their child to eat with the expression "a spoon for mommy, a spoon for daddy".[8] By appealing to the child's love of its parents, the seed is sown for the child to identify this love as part of itself. Clinical work with patients suffering from eating disorders clearly shows that this process does not always succeed. In these patients, the ego-drives collide with the sexual drives, and in the worst case, insufficient libidinal investment in the ego can lead to serious, life-threatening conditions. Patients suffering from eating disorders can deny themselves food as an expression of anger, frustration and grief over the inability to invest the ego, particularly the body ego, with sufficient libidinal energy. Patients with eating disorders have either been insufficiently mirrored, or they have been mirrored in an ambivalent or otherwise unsatisfactory way.

Narcissistic object choice differs from object choice by attachment in that the object is chosen as reflection of the idealised ego. Here, one strives to find oneself in the other, and one loves the person who mirrors and affirms one's self-image. Narcissistic object choice, wrote Freud, is typical of women, while men typically seek an object of attachment. Strictly speaking, a woman loves only herself in the same way as the man loves her. We must, however, attribute great importance to this type of woman in her love life, Freud continues. Such women exercise the strongest attraction on men, not only on aesthetic grounds, but as a consequence of particular psychological circumstances, and this is related to the fascination that a narcissistically self-sufficient person stirs up in one who has given up his own narcissism in the quest for an object of attachment.

To these observations I suggest adding a differentiation between what Freud termed "narcissistic object choice" and the narcissistically self-sufficient person. Allow me to expand the latter with reference to one of the artists who had a remarkable ability to portray women of self-contained beauty. The

Dutch painter Johannnes Vermeer (1632–1675) has, above any other painter, depicted women as resting in their own self-sufficient being. Vermeer's female figures radiate a rare intimacy. They see the viewer seeing them, but nevertheless remain at rest in their own activities and their own being. Whether they are fastening a necklace, pouring milk from a jug into a bowl or playing a musical instrument, Vermeer's female figures express the essence of femininity, the primordial image of the feminine, that they each and separately are materialisations of. Vermeer had the genius to depict the tranquil beauty of woman at rest in her own being.

Freud found the perfect example of this form of self-sufficiency in the child and termed it "primary narcissism". He assumed that the parents, in their love of the child, are mirrored in this primary narcissism and thus re-live and reproduce their own relinquished narcissism. The parents thus are prone to suspend all demands on the child that they have themselves been subjected to as a consequence of civilisation, and to wish for their children to enjoy all the privileges they have themselves lost. The modern term "helicopter parent" covers parents who attempt to eliminate all obstacles in the child's way, without understanding that it is their own lost narcissism that they are projecting into the image of a life without demands or restraints.

Besides the theme of love, it was the ego and its development that attracted Freud's attention during his work on the narcissism essay. The basic idea in Freud's essay, briefly expressed, is that narcissism is the libidinal cathexis of the self, but that this cathexis is effected through the ego and has crucial importance for the formation and development of the ego. To this, Freud adds the supposition that "a unity comparable to the ego cannot exist in the individual from the start; the ego has to be developed. The auto-erotic instincts, however, are there from the very first; so there must be something added to auto-erotism – a new psychical action – in order to bring about narcissism".[9] For the ego to initiate this development, a particular activity is necessary, which Freud understood as an unspecified form of identification, which occurs at such an early stage that there is as yet no clear discrimination of ego/self and object. The ego at this point coincides with the object, and difference is not recognised as such. This is primary narcissism, a short-lived condition in the development of the human child, after which every form of narcissism is secondary and is characterised by the ego withdrawing love from its objects and accumulating it in itself. An important aspect of the ego's development consists in the differentiation of the ego ideal which, as a secondary formation, constitutes a continuation of primary narcissism and has the important function of adapting the ego to the demands of cultural life. "What he projects before him as his ideal is the substitute for the lost narcissism of his childhood in which he was his own ideal".[10] Ego development consists in a distancing from primary narcissism, and this occurs, writes Freud, when libido is displaced onto culturally imposed ideals. In Freud, the concept of the ego ideal had particular significance, as it marked a turn from individual to social psychology. I will return to this after a brief presentation of the concept and phenomenon of narcissism after Freud.

As previously mentioned, narcissism remained a terminological parenthesis in Freud's work, a station on the way between his two drive theories. Freud himself was never to integrate his ideas on narcissism into the significant revision to which he subjected his drive theory, a few years later. The essay on narcissism, therefore, did not play a part in the decisive reworking of drive theory. It was Freud's successors who took up the concept of narcissism. For some, clinical observations of the different degrees of narcissistic disturbance made the phenomenon and concept important; for others, it was an attempt to integrate significant findings from the narcissism essay into the revised theory of the drives.

In clinical work, from the beginning of the 1970s, attention grew regarding a type of patient with a new kind of psychic disorder. Diagnostic manuals were altered, the diagnosis of personality disorder was introduced and patients with borderline or narcissistic personality disorder came to dominate the clinical picture of the period. The problematic of guilt was replaced by the problematic of shame, and clinical understanding was formulated in terms of disturbances of self-esteem, oscillating between omnipotence and inferiority.

In 1971, Heinz Kohut's ground-breaking book *The Analysis of the Self* was published and led to a breakthrough in the understanding of narcissism[11]. Kohut knew how the self-esteem of narcissistically disturbed patients oscillated between an omnipotent self and an idealised parental image. He also introduced the important concept of "selfobject" as an expression of the object or other not having a separate existence for the narcissist, but serving as a mirroring instance to stabilise the fragile self-esteem of the person in question. As a social and culture critical addition to Kohut's psychological description of narcissism, Christopher Lasch in 1979 published the book *The Culture of Narcissism*.[12] The book rapidly became a best-seller, which testifies to its importance in reflecting a new form of dependence in individuals in modern capitalist society, where bureaucratic dependency has replaced parental authority. This dependency creates not self-denial, but self-actualisation, not drive abstinence, but enjoyment, as Slavoj Žižek has expressed with his image of the obscene superego, the dictum of which is, in short: "Enjoy".[13] Lasch based his thesis of the decline of parental authority on a critical analysis of society, which to my mind needs to be complemented with an analysis of the symbolic discourse, which is mediated by language, myths and stories. The myth of Narcissus has, along with the myth of Oedipus, had major importance as a frame story of identity. Not so much because Oedipus' and Narcissus' fates were determined by the gods, or the oracle, but because these two legendary protagonists act in such ways that the words of the gods or oracle become real and understandable. Freud chose the myth of Oedipus, as he in it saw an image of a structure that could reflect the personality under the influence of a powerful paternal authority. When this authority crumbled, Narcissus took on the mytho-symbolical function and became the mirror of the extensive need for affirmation and appreciation of the exposed and fragile self.

In opposition to the extensive revision of psycho-analysis that took place in the United States under the influence of so-called ego psychology, French psycho-analysis had maintained interest in Freud's concept of narcissism. Lacan's introduction of the mirror metaphor, the order of the imaginary and his understanding of love built upon Freud's concepts, but complemented them by pointing to the destructive aspect of narcissism. Lacan[14] introduced the so-called "mirror stage", a concept which both expanded and revised some of Freud's ideas from the 1914 text. The concept of mirroring identification filled a gap with respect to the development of the ego, that Freud had not found a fitting concept for when he introduced the idea that the ego, and thus narcissism, are not present at the beginning of life, but emerge through an unspecified psychic act. Mirroring identification was the answer to this activity.

In general, narcissism refers to the imaginary relation between people. We mirror ourselves in the other and fall in love, like Narcissus, either with the idealised image of the other, or with the projection of our idealised ego, and this mirroring identification is not conceivable without aggressive aspects. Even if the mirror as instrument was used, not least by Lacan, to illustrate identification – particularly its imaginary aspect – it should not be understood too concretely, like Narcissus, gazing at his reflection in the lake. The image of the child in front of the mirror illustrates something that reaches far beyond the mirror itself. We mirror ourselves in the gaze of the other, which implies that this other will always be present as a precipitate in the subject. The outline of the other is part of the subject's or ego's development. At the heart of identity, or the ego, there will thus always be an element of alienation, coinciding with the outline of the other. As self-reflective beings, our selves always stand in relation to something within us that is other than the self. Kierkegaard has expressed it thus: "The self is a relation that relates itself to itself or is the relation's relating itself to itself".[15] Jean-Paul Sartre, in *Being and Nothingness,*[16] writes that the gaze of the other is the intermediary that brings one back to oneself, and that one only discovers oneself by being seen by the other. Paul Ricoeur has developed the same thought in his book *Oneself as Another.*[17] It is, however, Lacan who is to be credited for pointing out that the internal relation between the self and the other includes the possibility of the other adopting what Lacan[18] has termed "the master discourse". The doubling of the self then takes the form of a mutually exclusive relation, in the sense that it's "either him or me". The other, in the guise of "him" does not necessarily refer to the concrete other, but to the position we allow the other to occupy within the area where we reflectively, in judgement or praise, relate to ourselves. Thus, we notice the splinter dwelling in our eye, and direct evil and hate towards ourselves, as if it came from a concrete other. And when convinced that the root of evil is in the other that offends or rejects us, this is often a projection of the other living within us.

Lacan[19] took Ovid's description of Narcissus' fate literally and spoke of "narcissistically suicidal aggression". He thus underlined that the erotic-aggressive character of narcissistic immersion into one's own reflection can lead the subject towards self-destructiveness, just as Narcissus and his tragic fate demonstrate. This destructive aspect of narcissism has been actualised in light of the many instances of serious psychic suffering that we see today, which have previously not been sufficiently understood. Examples of these are self-destructive behaviour, anorexia, psychosomatic illness and serious states of depression. Instead of viewing these self-destructive actions as expressions of a speculative theory of the death drive, it has been more fruitful to understand them within the narcissistic spectrum. Here, it is not a question of libidinal investment of the ego, but on the contrary, a quest for the dissolution of every form of tension, a striving towards what Freud termed Nirvana, a sort of existential nothingness. It is a state of which many patients speak, where they, attempting to numb psychic pain, strive to annul all internal tension through various self-destructive acts, in order not to feel. This eventually leads to feelings of annihilation and inner emptiness.[20]

Let us lastly return to Freud and his concept of the ego ideal, which was to become an important piece in the puzzle of the narcissism of social life, and which, to my mind, might add an important and critical view of contemporary events. The ego ideal became an important cultural factor, not least in Freud's studies of group psychology and ego analysis.[21] The impetus for the formation of the ego ideal is to be found in the critical influence of the parents, which is later taken over by social institutions and by the groups that contextualise the life of the individual. In our time, the use of social media has become an important contribution to the mirroring on which the formation and development of the ego ideal depends.

The ego ideal is also the common ideal of a family, a class or a nation. But since the ego ideal was understood as a displaced expression of the self-love we needed as children, we can expect, writes Freud, to find narcissistic elements in the ideals that bind people together, beginning with the family, followed by race, religion, nation and finally in that great unity called humankind. It is love that's binds people to each other, but in its idealised and sexually inhibited form. The survival of a group or mass crucially depends on whether aim-inhibited sexuality can be sublimated into the affection which is essential to every group's cohesion. Once in a while, we are reminded that such inhibition and sublimation surpass what a human being is capable of, and we see examples of sexual violation of children in precisely the institutions which should protect them.

What psychoanalysis has studied in the individual's libidinal development can be also be found in social groups. Libido is linked to the ego-drives and chooses the persons that support these as its objects of love, and just as in the case of the individual, it is love that limits self-love in the development of humankind, and promotes development from egotism to altruism. It should, however, come neither as a surprise nor a cause for indignation that the loss of narcissism leads to demarcations towards groups that are foreign to the group one is oneself a part of. As ego-drives and sexual drives are bound together and mutually support each other, humans do not fight each other only for the sake of survival, but also out of narcissistic love for the ego and the resulting hostility toward the object; the other or others. In *Civilization and its Discontents,*[22] Freud introduced the term "narcissism of small differences" as the expression of the antipathy or hostility existing between groups living in proximity to each other, neighbours or parts of a country, which have become resentful adversaries, and where each party regards itself as better and more worthy than the rival. In larger groups, created on the grounds of race, religion or nation, the small differences become the narcissism of large differences, and we see irrefutable evidence that self-love and narcissism assert themselves and signal that departures from the ideal of the own group constitutes a threat that must be fought. Thus, humans defend themselves with the arrogance of narcissistic offence and the devaluation of foreign cultures, races and religions. When the culturally or religiously foreign, as part of such a defence, is expressed in stereotypes of them and us, there is a threat to the sense of community, and the path is opened to negative and destructive aspects of narcissism, which contain the hate and disdain for that which, in the same movement, becomes foreign in the negative sense.

Notes

1 Ovid. (1922). *Metamorphoses*, book 3, 435. Translated by Brookes More. Boston: Cornhill Publishing Co.
2 Freud, S. (1914). On Narcissism: An Introduction. *The Standard Edition of the Psychological Works of Sigmund Freud*, Vol. XIV. London: The Hogarth Press.
3 Kierkegaard, S. (1849/1983). *The Sickness Unto Death*. Translated by H.V. Hong & E.V. Hong. Princeton, New Jersey: Princeton University Press.
4 Zupančič, A. (2000). *Ethics of the Real. Kant and Lacan*. London: Verso.
5 Freud, S. (1910). Leonardo da Vinci and a Memory from his Childhood. *The Standard Edition of the Psychological Works of Sigmund Freud*, Vol. XI. London: The Hogarth Press.
6 Freud, S. (1911) Psycho-Analytic Notes on an Autobiographical Account of a Case of Paranoia. *The Standard Edition of the Psychological Works of Sigmund Freud*, Vol. XII. London: The Hogarth Press.
7 Freud, S. (1914). On Narcissism: An Introduction. *The Standard Edition of the Psychological Works of Sigmund Freud*, Vol. XIV, p. 82. London: The Hogarth Press.
8 Laplanche, J. (1970/1985). *Life and Death in Psychoanalysis*, p. 83. Translated by Jeffrey Mehlman. Baltimore: Johns Hopkins University Press.
9 Freud, S. (1914). On Narcissism: An Introduction. *The Standard Edition of the Psychological Works of Sigmund Freud*, Vol. XIV, p. 77. London: The Hogarth Press.
10 Freud, S. (1914). On Narcissism: An Introduction. *The Standard Edition of the Psychological Works of Sigmund Freud*, Vol. XIV, p. 94. London: The Hogarth Press.
11 Kohut, H. (1971). *The Analysis of the Self: A Systematic Approach to the Psychoanalytic Tratment of Narcissistic Personality Disorders*. New York: International Universities Press.
12 Lasch, C. (1979). *The Culture of Narcissism. American Life in an Age of Diminishing Expectations*. New York: W. W. Norton.

13 Žižek, S. (1994). *The Metastases of Enjoyment. On Women and Causality*. New York: Verso.
14 Lacan, J. (1966). *Écrits*, pp. 75–82. London: W.W. Norton & Company.
15 Kierkegaard, S. (1849/1980). *The Sickness Unto Death*, p. 13. Translated by H.V. Hong & E.V. Hong. Princeton, New Jersey: Princeton University Press.
16 Sartre, J.-P. (1943/1992). *Being and Nothingness. A Phenomenological Essay on Ontology*. Translated by Hazel E. Barnes. New York: Simon & Schuster.
17 Ricoeur, P. (1990). *Oneself as Another*. Chicago: The University of Chicago Press.
18 Lacan, J. (1981). *The Psychoses. The Seminar of Jacques Lacan*. Book III, pp. 92–97. London: Routledge.
19 Lacan, J. (1966). *Écrits*, p. 174, 187. London: W.W. Norton & Company.
20 Cf. Green, A. (2001). *Life Narcissism, Death Narcissism*. London: Free Association Books; Laplanche, J. (2011): *Freud and the Sexual*. New York: International Psychoanalytic Books; de M'Uzan, M. (2013). *Death and Identity. Being and the Psycho-Sexual Drama*. London: Karnac.
21 Freud, S. (1921). Group Psychology and the Analysis of the Ego. *The Standard Edition of the Psychological Works of Sigmund Freud,* Vol. XVIII, pp. 65–144. London: The Hogarth Press.
22 Freud, S. (1930). Civilization and its Discontents. *The Standard Edition of the Psychological Works of Sigmund Freud,* Vol. XXI. London: The Hogarth Press.

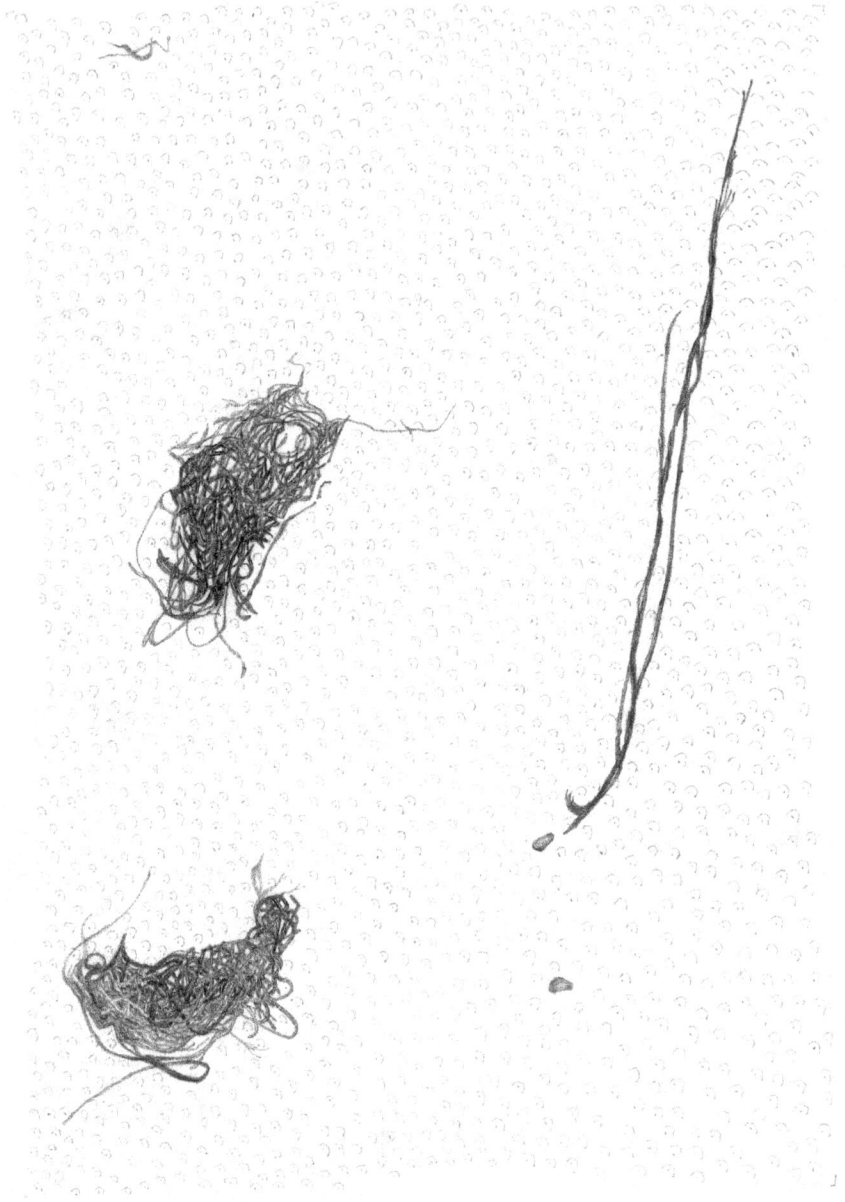

Chapter 6

On the symptom

By way of introduction to this essay, I will briefly touch upon a subject related to the symptom, namely that of diagnosis. Diagnoses are made on the basis of symptoms, and besides being intimately connected, diagnoses and symptoms share some common problems.

When I, in connection with my supervision of psychologists in the psychiatric wards of hospitals, experience to what extent diagnoses fill the work of psychiatrists, I at times feel downcast. Diagnoses are indispensable tools, and there is no doubt that diagnostic systems have been refined over time, and that psychiatrists as well as psychologists have lengthy experience in using them, to the great benefit of their patients. Nonetheless, it is worth noting that diagnoses, like symptoms, are semantic phenomena, and since they both belong to the domain of concepts, are subordinate to socio-cultural conventions, with the limitations this entails. A diagnosis is not identical to the underlying symptom, nor with the person diagnosed. The more sophisticated and diversified diagnoses become, the better psychiatrists and psychologists become at giving factual and rational explanations to the hidden illness. Correspondingly, the question is raised of how to understand the relation between the diagnosis and the person diagnosed. Here, rational explanations are of no avail, for the simple reason that we encounter the irrational aspects of the subject. Diagnoses are a way of looking resulting from conclusions about processes and phenomena belonging to an invisible and often inexplicable world, be it the internal world of the body or the internal psychic world. It seems absurd that a person can receive up to six different diagnoses, which was the instance when I last supervised the case of a young hospitalised woman. It is remarkable that a diagnosis can occupy so much of the fore-ground, that it is difficult to catch sight of the person behind it. I have had the same disturbing experience when supervising students who, at the first supervisory meeting, introduced themselves with a diagnosis, for example, saying "I am bipolar" or "I am borderline". I answered them that this was good for me to know, but that first I would like to know their name and what they expected from the supervision.

There is no doubt that for some, receiving a diagnosis can be a relief, even if it is a psychiatric diagnosis. But a diagnosis can also easily become a façade, held up as a protective shield. When handled like calling cards, or in a way where person and diagnosis collapse into one, diagnoses exceed their conceptual context, and we forget the distance between signifier and signified, which in this case is a human being. Diagnoses are made on the basis of symptoms or symptomatology, and symptoms, as well as diagnoses, are signs speaking of disturbance. Symptoms being signs means that they, along with diagnoses, call for reading and interpretation.

Long before the advent of modern medicine, and also long before Hippocrates laid the grounds of contemporary medicine, man speculated on the origin of the harsh reality of human suffering. Hesiod – the first didactic poet in Greek literary tradition, took up this question and tried to answer it mythologically. In the past, he writes, humans were not plagued by work or by suffering. The earth gave an abundance of food, and humans lived in harmony with the gods. This, however, changed when Prometheus, in the service of humans, challenged Zeus' omnipotence. The god was so angered that he withdrew fire from humanity, but Prometheus stole it back. Zeus' answer was not to take gifts from humanity – but to give them gifts in the form of numerous torments, brought from Pandora's "infamous" box. Since then, illness has ravaged humanity, befalling it in silence, since Zeus deprived it of a voice.[1]

The philosopher Plutarch had a more rational approach to human suffering. He corrected Hesiod's idea on the silence of suffering and made the point that although the ailment remained hidden, precursors such as exhaustion or digestive troubles could be observed, presaging the arrival of illness, and could be read as signs or symptoms of invisible disease. Plutarch thus abandoned the archaic understanding of illness as inner daemons and replaced it with the assumption of processes covertly unfolding within the body. Despite their different approaches to the symptom, Hesiod and Plutarch were preoccupied with the same problem: finding out where symptoms came from and how to read them. A symptom is a disturbance without visible cause, but often accompanied by pain. The symptom thus indicates an invisible dimension of our being, which can, however, be made available. For the archaic world as well as for our contemporary one, the symptom has challenged the human intellect to find logical and rational interpretations for it. As the symptom can include serious violations of a subject's boundaries, it engages not only our intellect, but also our creativity and invites us to imagine invisible agents and forces, capable of so much damage. Correspondingly, it is not surprising that the archaic idea of daemons has survived. A modern doctor such as Freud used the adjective daemonic for the repetition compulsion which characterised certain symptoms. Even today, the word *daemonic* is an eloquent expression of the strange and irrational actions committed by humans beyond their conscious knowledge.

Since the Hippocratic canon, medical science has developed greater knowledge of the hidden functions and disturbances of the body, and some techniques to intervene and ultimately cure diseases.

It was the strangeness of the body, its manifold disturbances driven by invisible forces, and not least the representations of its impersonal and inhuman character, that inspired interest in the psyche during the archaic and classical periods. Through its affinity to the body, the psyche was eventually attributed the same daemonic powers, posing medical science before new challenges, simultaneously as the psychic became the inspiration for the tragedians, among them Euripides, the youngest of the tragedians to make the human psyche enter the scene of tragedy, creating the psychological drama. When we speak of the body as soma, we presuppose the existence of something that is not soma, which we call the soul, psyche or subject. In one of Plato's earliest dialogues, he attributes this idea to Alcibiades, letting him say that since the body cannot use or rule itself; something else must rule it. While in Homeric times the psyche was regarded only as that which deserts us and disappears when we die, it was the evolution of classical medicine and its study of the body and its disturbances that created interest in the human psyche. But although Hippocratic medical science in the late Hellenistic period had greatly progressed, particularly in the somatic domain, the symptom remained strange. More than a thousand years later, Freud wrote that the symptom is the most ego-alien phenomenon we can encounter. This strangeness has given rise to a host of conclusions on underlying causes, despite the interpretation of some of these symptoms through modern science. The prime example is the hysterical symptom, throughout our cultural history regarded as a specifically feminine symptom, which is underscored by its name, a paraphrase of "hysteron", the Greek term for the womb. In *Timaeus,* Plato illustrated the idea of the particular affinity of hysteria to woman and her life-giving organ, the womb, in an amusing tale which is not devoid of insight. He first describes the male genitals and writes that they are naturally disobedient and wilful, furiously attempting to dominate all things. "Much of the same is true of the matrix or womb in women, which is a living creature within them which long to bear children. And if it is left unfertilized long beyond the normal time, it causes extreme unrest, strays about the body, blocks the channels of breath and causes in consequence acute distress and disorders of all kinds".[2]

Plato's idea survived within cultural history. As late as in Charcot, the French doctor famous for his treatment of hysterical patients, we find the same reasoning although the womb is here replaced by the ovaries as the disruptive organ – to Charcot's male gaze. As a consequence, Charcot invented the so-called ovary compressor, which was applied to the outside of a woman's abdomen to press the ovaries into place. Freud gradually replaced this fantastic story by another way of reading the symptom, as he learned to listen to his hysterical patient's complaints and thus experienced that behind the symptom hid neither gods nor daemons but wretched sexual and love lives. Like

Plutarch, Freud understood that symptoms require reading and interpretation. It was through his work with primarily hysterical patients that Freud developed his theory and introduced a method of treatment that relied exclusively on speech. Psychoanalysis became a "talking cure". But not only did Freud listen to his patients; he also learned to *read* their symptoms. He thus elaborated the tradition founded by Plutarch, among others.

A look at Freud's early work on hysteria shows how he, through his patient's speech, learned to understand the meaning concealed within the symptoms, and to read these like a text that could be decoded and interpreted in the same way as the particular language of dreams. Characteristic for hysterical suffering are bodily symptoms in the form of pain, cramps, pareses, disturbances of vision, etc., lacking somatic cause but indicating that the patient has converted psychic suffering or pain and given it bodily expression. One of Freud's patients, Frau Cäcilie M., suffered from acute pains on one side of her face, which she herself interpreted as an expression of her husband's behaviour being like a slap in the face. At another point she felt a sharp pain in her head, which she brought back to an event when a relative had given her a piercing look. Another patient limped as an expression of having committed a sexual faux pas. A third patient suffered from paralysis of the legs, and with this symptom expressed that she could not stand on her own feet. The hysterical symptom departs from verbal expressions like manners of speech or statements best understood as dead metaphors. Expressions such as a piercing gaze or a slap in the face are originally metaphors which, due to frequent use, have lost their power, slipped into common language, and become figures of speech. The hysteric brings them back to life by placing her vexations and thwarted passions in them. The hysterical symptom is the dramatic expression of repressed passion, created by the use of rhetoric tropes, in this case the metaphor. By listening to the speech accompanying the symptoms, Freud could shed light on the functioning and disturbances of the psyche and thus solve the enigma of the soma's relation to the psyche, a problem with which the ancient Greeks wrestled in their attempts to reach beyond the body or soma.

Besides hysteria, obsessional neurosis set the foundation for the psychoanalytic theory of the evolution of the psychic symptom, and while hysteria made use of metaphor as a path to the symptom, it was metonymy, or displacement, that was manifested in obsessions and compulsions. Today, the diagnosis "obsessional neurosis" is no longer used. It has been replaced by the term "OCD", which stands for "obsessive-compulsive disorder". Here, however, something essential is lost. The diagnosis OCD is a good example of how a diagnosis collapses into the illness, reducing the distance between the diagnosis and the complicated suffering behind it.

The term OCD suggests that the theory of symptom-development has completely slipped out of the diagnosis, which is purely observational and descriptive of behaviour. This equally entails that the preferential treatment, in accordance with the above, is cognitive and behaviourally corrective, aiming to remove symptoms and reduce anxiety. But as Freud writes, nothing is achieved by the removal of one symptom except clearing the path for a new one. In the following, I will attempt to penetrate behind the symptom and describe the mechanisms responsible for the formation of symptoms. A case of obsessional neurosis will serve as illustration.

A man in his forties turned to me when the psychiatrist he consulted had given up further treatment. At our first meeting, expressing shame and guilt, he told me that he suffered from a urine phobia that had thrown him into cleaning rituals that had paralysed his life. Going to the toilet entailed a risk of "contamination" from urine. This gifted man was fully aware that urine is relatively harmless, but in his fantasy, urine had the character of a contagious substance capable of inflicting serious damage and, not least, decomposing his brain, leading to his dissolution. After visits to the toilet, the fantasy of possible internal dissolution led him to extensive washing not only of his body but of clothes, belt, credit card and whatever else he was carrying. About the history of his illness, he told me that it had appeared at a time when he was preparing his final examinations in high school, and that the first sign was a thought of which he was unable to free himself. He was "anxious of not being able to concentrate at the thought of not being able to concentrate". This obsession manifests the characteristic mark of the obsessional, who attempts to displace the complex problematic he suffers from to an ideational level. The obsessional can thus appear a caricature of enlightened rationality. "Cogito ergo sum". Like the rationalist, the obsessional has created an autarchy of thinking, and this insistence on the omnipotence of thoughts presents one of the greatest difficulties in the work with these patients. It is, however, important not to overlook the aspect of resistance, which hides in the remarkably detailed descriptions of compulsions, that these patients insist on telling and re-telling. Something is kept out, and this something is related to pleasure, as we will see. The Slovenian philosopher Mladen Dolar, in his article on the uncanny *I Shall Be with You on Your Wedding-Night*, suggests that obsessional neurosis shares features with the uncanny, which consist in the absence of insecurity or doubt; in both cases, it is a question of "too much certainty, when escape through hesitation is no longer possible, when the object comes too close".[3] This formulation, I believe, quite precisely captures the intensity of anxiety as well as the patient's conviction of the reality of danger.

As a psychoanalyst, one asks oneself the same question as the layman: What makes people act so irrationally, going through such pains? As psychoanalysts, we know that analysis can only hope to answer this question. But we sense that the answer lies in a particular kind of pleasure at the heart of the symptom, beyond language and meaning.

In conclusion of his most comprehensive text on the technique of treatment, Freud[4] writes that after the termination of analysis "there are nearly always residual phenomena". In other words, there is something the talking cure cannot translate into words, and which is difficult to incorporate into language. This does not imply that the symptom lacks meaning. In general, symptoms belong to the symbolic order and are therefore available to understanding. But the symptom is also intimately tied to the physical body, with the real and with the pleasure linked to the body, not least through the erogenous zones – oral, anal and genital – and this pleasure creates the greatest resistance to change.

In his two lectures on the symptom, Freud has followed these two paths. In the first lecture, *The Sense of Symptoms*, just as the title indicates, he treats the meaning of the symptom, while the following lecture, *The Paths to the Formation of Symptoms,*[5] explores how the drive, concealed in the symptom, follows its way to gratification. For Freud, and later for Jacques Lacan, French psychoanalyst and today one of Freud's most important successors, the exploration of the symptom revolves around connecting these two aspects, the aspect which, through interpretation, allows the manifestation of a concealed or repressed meaning, and the one that lies beyond meaning but nevertheless can be articulated and bring coherence to the meaning of the symptom. I will try to illustrate these two roads to understanding the symptom's meaning and signification through the analytic work with my analysand.

Central to the analysand's obsessions and compulsions was a fantasy of annihilation if he came into contact with urine. We found certain meaning in this fantasy by linking it to some particular features of his history. Through his material, it occurred to me that it was his mother's fate he, so to speak, lived in his own body. The mother was hospitalised and had been operated for a brain tumour when he was rather young, and throughout his childhood, he was terrified by his mother who, calling and shouting, would stagger through the rooms of their home. The father, a physician and authoritative, God-fearing person, explained to the panic-stricken boy that this was due to the brain tumour, and urged him to have compassion with the mother. It was many years later that the analysand understood the real circumstances. Beneath his command, the father concealed the truth, namely the mother's alcohol abuse, a truth that became obvious to my analysand much later. At the time when the first obsessive thought appeared, he developed a disorder of vision that prevented him from studying and eventually graduating from high school, pointing to an identification with the mother's illness. At the same point in time, he had suggested that the father terminate the mother's life and put an end to her suffering. He thus turned the command of compassion imposed by his father against the latter and could, in this way, express the anger, frustration and despair that the inexplicable and secret family situation had provoked in him.

The seed of the urine phobia and compulsive rituals was linked to an accidental event, at a point in time when he had left home. One day when he was on his way from a laundry, his clean clothes brushed against a drunk man. The smell of this man, which he associated to urine, sent him into a panic, and he returned to the laundry and washed his clothes once more. The smell of urine was linked to the mother and tied to a distinct memory. The mother had borrowed one of his coats, and when she returned it, a smell clung to it, which he claimed was the odour of urine. The smell emanating from his mother, mistakenly interpreted as that of urine, was thus the gravitational centre of the fantasy of annihilation which had frightened him throughout childhood, and was manifested in his first obsessional symptoms, when he while studying for his examinations, and because of the turbulent family situation fell ill with obsessional neurosis. We had thus uncovered a measure of meaning in his symptoms. Much was, however, still unclear, in particular the insistence and perseverance of his symptom. What were the forces that continued to compel my patient to these endless washing rituals?

Throughout the many years of analysis, I became well acquainted with the extensive washing rituals he imposed on himself as a form of bodily cleansing and act of contrition for disgraceful or unpardonable behaviour. In the form of magical thinking, my patient resorted to a means that has always been used by human beings, for instance, in penance for murder. Thus, Ulysses quite literally was compelled to cleanse himself of sin and bloodshed when he, after returning home from his long voyage, had murdered Penelope's suitors, and ill people in ancient Greece had to perform ablutions before journeying into holy cities devoted to the god of healing, Asclepius. This magical form of thinking is frequently used by children in play as well as when they are anxious and never entirely disappears but can, as a consequence of anxiety, reappear and serve to ward off imagined catastrophes. My analysand suffered from panic attacks whenever the soiling fantasy threatened him, and he had no resort other than bodily cleansing. It gave him momentary relief, which was however soon replaced by profound shame, an expression of the humiliation suffered by his ego through the imposition of the washing rituals. What was in question was not only anxiety, shame and guilt, but also a particular kind of pleasure. I could, in my analysand, notice a striking contrast between the carelessness surrounding his micturition and the conscientiousness with which he performed the following washing rituals.

One day, something happened which was to have decisive meaning for the following work and which manifested the gratification which was part of the symptom. My analysand had, from the beginning of the treatment, made use of the toilet before as well as after our sessions, and with time I couldn't help noticing the unmistakable smell of urine in the toilet used by my patients. I brought this up with him and suggested that there for him might be a particular form of pleasure connected with urination. To my surprise, he promptly answered my interpretation by saying that he often played with the thought of "pissing on his most beloved books" and that he could feel horror mixed with pleasure at the thought of letting the toilet brush touch his most exquisite writing instruments. We had thus moved in the direction of understanding the particular kind of pleasure hidden deepest in the symptom, covered by shame and guilt. This pleasure, which has a sadistic character in the obsessional, is difficult to access. Nonetheless, it is decisive for the treatment that it is articulated and linked to the fantasies, and the meaning that can be read in these. The psychoanalytic assumption of the hidden sadistic pleasure of the obsessional is linked to the concept of regression, which is one of the main concepts in Freud's lecture on the formation of the symptom.[6] Regression refers to the drive returning to earlier forms of satisfaction under the pressure of sexual frustration later in life. Regression can take two forms, either a return to an earlier sexual object in consequence of disappointment or feelings of abandonment, or a return to earlier forms of satisfaction. While the hysteric typically regresses to an earlier object, the obsessional reverts to an earlier mode of satisfaction, which is frequently the pleasure of the anal-sadistic phase. We can thus trace the pleasure that, fixated to a particular bodily zone, plays an important part in obsessional neurosis. The concealed pleasure of the obsessional is linked to his symptoms and hidden within his fantasies, and therefore gives a rare insight into the patient's infantile and perverse sexuality, helping us understand why these patients find it so difficult to give up symptomatic drive gratification despite the suffering that accompanies it. To a great extent, Lacan contributed in demonstrating the underlying ambiguity of the symptom. The symptom is, according to Lacan, a symbolic construction built around a real kernel consisting of pleasure, corresponding, in Freud's words, to the grain of sand around which the mussel makes its pearl.[7]

Lacan has suggested that within the depth of our intimacy is an ex-timacy – a remains never taken up into the symbolical order. Even if this remainder is not available to meaning and signification, it is the task of psychoanalysis to articulate it, and to integrate it into a meaningful context. It is work on the analysand's fantasies that allows an articulation of this remainder while simultaneously demonstrating how the analysand organises his enjoyment or jouissance.

It is characteristic of every neurosis that regardless of how disturbing and paralysing the symptom, the neurosis is, after all, limited. The analysand had, as he said, a happy marriage and satisfying sexual life. He had three well-functioning children, a job he valued, and in his free time enjoyed painting and reading all kinds of literature. In contrast, the symptom lived its own life. On the symptomatic level, it was not his phallus or genital that was in question, but rather his wee-wee. Here he had deposited the fantasy of annihilation through the contagious substance along with his anxiety, guilt and shame, and only the compulsive cleansing ritual could momentarily calm his anxiety. It is important to be aware that the bodily part where the symptom took root was not verbally available. The symptom had, on the contrary, acquired a thing-like character. In other words, a de-symbolisation or de-signification had taken place. This could explain the mechanical quality of the symptom. It acts, so to speak, beyond the intervention of consciousness. In his seminar on anxiety related to obsessional neurosis, Lacan[8] uses the metaphor of a dripping faucet, while my analysand explained that it was as if he had a four-lane motorway in his brain in connection to something constantly insisting on being realised, something frightening as well as pleasurable. This mechanical quality is what gives obsessional neurosis its daemonic and uncanny character, and it was precisely this mechanical aspect of the psyche that made Freud speak of unbound energy, an energy not woven into a semantic context, and of a compulsion to repeat, that is, a repetition beyond the control of the will.

In obsessional neurosis, there is a paradoxical form of mental energy that leaves the subject locked and paralysed, or with an expression from American scholar Eric Santner,[9] we can speak of an intensification, a too-muchness or unavailable excess which can only be slightly alleviated by being displaced to rigid patterns of repetition. This too-muchness can be seen in the repetition compulsion, which knows no limits and will not be curbed by considerations of reality or the subject. The most widely known example of this excessive element is intoxication, but also people addicted to sexual stimulation manifest this too-muchness as they nearly become slaves of repetition and of intense excitement.

Despite the seeming mechanical character of obsessional neurosis, we do not find ourselves outside the realm of the psychic, or of meaning or signification, and even if the compulsions, to the person performing them, seem devoid of meaning, there is no doubt that they possess meaning. The difference between having a significance and being significant was something I had occasion to learn when my analysand, the first day after a long holiday, telephoned to say he was feeling so ill that he would prefer to cancel next day's scheduled session. When I understood that he was not physically ill, I suggested that it might help him to come to the session, which he did, and told me that during the holiday, he had felt terrible anxiety of being contaminated by urine, and as his wife this time refused to participate in the washing rituals, his anxiety multiplied. At this point, he thought of the Dictaphone he had used one day when anxiety overwhelmed him, and he had been unable to tell me, and recorded the scenario of anxiety, asking me to keep the Dictaphone. His idea was now that the Dictaphone could be contaminated, and his anxiety was displaced to it. I could register a certain pressure within me, not because of the story of the Dictaphone, but because I noticed that his narration contained a demand, or plea. I conveyed this to him, and he answered, confirming my interpretation, that "he knew, that I would not clean it for him".

This statement can be interpreted as a wish that I could be persuaded to adopt his wife's function, but it might also be that he harboured a wish that I would participate in his symptom on a level beyond the verbal, and finally, that I might be able to touch the "contaminated" thing and thus prove its harmlessness.

When helping people with such remarkable and mechanical behaviour patterns, it is important to keep in mind that there is meaning in the madness. There is a measure of demand or desire in the symptom that we can register as well as make meaningful by linking the isolated somatic symptoms to the analysand's fantasies. The demand originates in a fixation in form of a bodily enjoyment which is not immediately inscribable or understandable within meaningful discourse. Nonetheless, the body, like the dream speaks, but in a language the words and grammar of which we must learn, as Freud writes in his *Interpretation of Dreams*.[10] In this text, he brings our attention to the fact that our interpretation of a dream or symptom encounters a resistance, for which Freud coined the term "the navel of the dream", the place where the dream is fastened to the unknown, an admission that there exists, beyond language and meaning, an end-point to the verbal understanding of the dream or symptom.

While Freud speaks of working through as a way of bringing the language of the symptom into analytic work, Lacan uses the expression traversing the fantasy. It was the toilet episode that opened the way to the wish to "piss on his books", and from this point, we could begin to unfold the fantasies linked to this. It was as if the task consisted in almost concretely severing the enjoyment from its bodily place of fixation and leading it into the domain of meaning. For a long time, we worked on his fear of and anger at his father. As a boy and later a young man, my analysand was surrounded by messages he could not understand. But he understood that something was utterly mad and assumed that the father had the privilege and right to judge the, to the boy, seemingly inexplicable circumstances that reigned in his home. He was in awe of the father's judgement. When he, in high school, read the Danish poet Kaj Munk's *The Word*,[11] it was a revelation of the secret troubles and inexplicable deeds of the people closest to him, who were troubled by something they did not understand themselves. *The Word* was thus a manifestation of a God he could associate to his father. It was a cruel God, a Jahve-God.

Behind these oedipal thoughts and fantasies circulating around the "Law of the Father" lay a deeper and less accessible layer of fantasies linked to the mother. The first obsession, of not being able to concentrate at the thought of not being able to concentrate, and the following disorder of vision naturally brought to mind the mother's illness, when he was quite young and in an early, affective identification with her. He had, so to speak, incorporated the brain tumour that his mother had been treated for, and had, on a pre-verbal level, made it a fantasy about his own fate. It was only under the pressure of his final examinations that this unrepresented thing, this inaccessible layer within him manifested itself, and he incarnated the mother's illness in his own body. Through the many years of work on different psychic levels, we were to a certain extent able to free the symptom from its bodily fixation, and he experienced relief from anxiety, shame and guilt. Throughout the duration of our work, I learned how important it is to look behind the diagnosis as well as the symptom, and that treatment that only aims at the remission of symptoms and their accompanying anxiety never reaches its goal. Instead of focusing on the symptom, I propose to look at both the symptom and the anxiety as a window through which one glimpses the hidden cause and pleasure.

Notes

1 Based on Holmes, B. (2010). *The Symptom and the Subject*. Princeton, New Jersey: Princeton University Press.
2 Plato. (1971). *Timaeus and Critias*, p. 120. London: Penguin Books.
3 Dolar, M. (1991). "I Shall Be with You on Your Wedding-Night". Lacan and the Uncanny. *October*, Vol. 58, p. 23.
4 Freud, S. (1937). Analysis Terminable and Interminable. *The Standard Edition of the Complete Psychological Works of Sigmund Freud*, Vol. XXIII, p. 228. London: The Hogarth Press.
5 Freud, S. (1916–1917). The Sense of Symptoms and The Paths to the Formation of Symptoms. In: Introductory Lectures on Psycho-Analysis. *The Standard Edition of the Complete Psychological Works of Sigmund Freud*, Vol. XV. London: The Hogarth Press.
6 Freud, S. (1916–1917). The Paths to the Formation of Symptoms. In: Introductory Lectures on Psycho-Analysis. *The Standard Edition of the Complete Psychological Works of Sigmund Freud*, Vol. XV. London: The Hogarth Press.
7 Freud, S. (1905). Fragments of an Analysis of a Case of Hysteria. *The Standard Edition of the Complete Psychological Works of Sigmund Freud*, Vol. VII, p. 83. London: The Hogarth Press.
8 Lacan, J. (2004/2016). *Anxiety. The Seminar of Jacques Lacan*, Book X. Cambridge: Polity Press.
9 Santner, E. (2001). *On the Psychotheology of Everyday Life*. Chicago: The University of Chicago Press.
10 Freud, S. (1900). The Interpretation of Dreams. *The Standard Edition of the Complete Psychological Works of Sigmund Freud*, Vol. IV. London: The Hogarth Press.
11 Munk, K. (1932). *The Word* (Danish: Ordet). Kaj Munk (1893–1944) was a Danish playwright, priest and patriot. *The Word* is a miracle play set among Jutland peasants, which established him as one of Denmark's leading dramatists. Munk often chose a dictator or "strong man" whom he showed as vainly struggling against God.

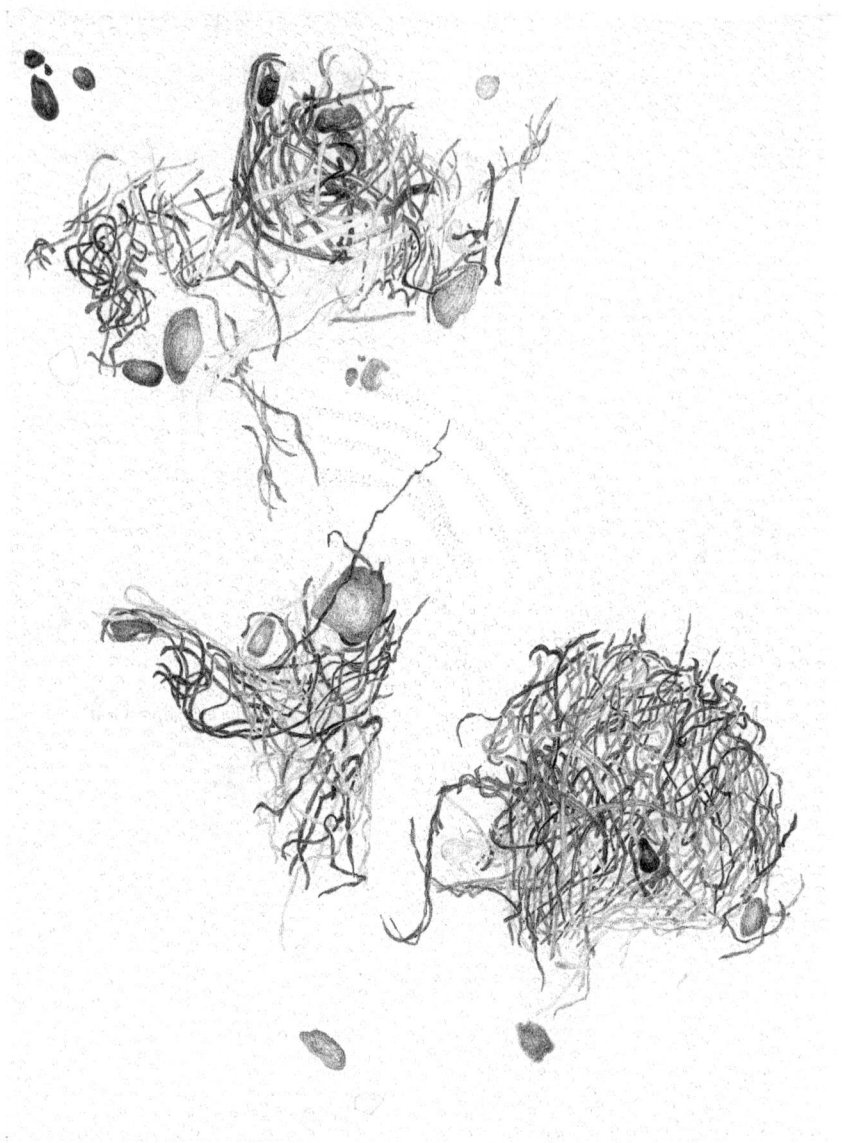

Chapter 7

Why war?

It attracts attention when two of the most ingenious thinkers of the 20th century exchange letters on war and attempt to explain the cruelty and horror that have accompanied the history of human civilisation, indeed have been an inevitable part of it. The correspondence between Albert Einstein and Sigmund Freud in 1932 has become famous, and has been commented and discussed. It came into being at the request of the League of Nations and the International Institute of Intellectual Co-operation, who had asked Einstein to discuss a problem of his choice with a person esteemed to possess the knowledge and insight necessary for a response. On the 30th of July 1932, Einstein wrote to Freud, asking him whether it was possible to free humans from the menace of war.[1]

Freud's reply to Einstein is marked by his lack of enthusiasm for the task, which to him seemed "tedious and sterile". One intuits a certain impatience and an unambiguous dissatisfaction with the contribution he was able to make. The two men did not have a close relationship. They had met only once. Of this meeting, Freud had said, with a certain ironic distance, that although Einstein understood psychology as little as he understood physics, they had had an agreeable conversation.

Freud's hesitant, and as he expresses it himself, rather insufficient reply did not imply that the subject did not occupy him. On the contrary, war, and not least the intimate relationship between war and death, were consistent themes in Freud's writings, and shortly after the First World War, received independent consideration in *Thoughts for the Times on War and Death*.[2] Here, Freud expresses his disillusioned attitude towards time and the belief in world progress. It is possible that this disenchantment played a part in the hesitant approach that can be read in his reply to Einstein, which contrasts with the resolute and unequivocal stance that Einstein expressed in his request to Freud.

Einstein opens by sketching the dimensions of the problem, thus revealing himself as a critical observer of his time. If the riches of the world, he says, were more justly distributed, and if we worked constructively, refusing to be misled into preparation for new wars, and struggled only for what is worth the

struggle, which is not imaginary border, prejudices or greed disguised as pa-
triotism, we might be able to give every human being a worthy life. He
continues admitting that "the normal objective of my thought affords no
insight into the dark places of human will and feeling, Tus in the enquiry now
proposed, I can do little more than seek to clarify the question at issue and,
clearing the ground of the more obvious solutions, enable you to bring the
light of your far-reaching knowledge of man's instinctive life to bear upon the
problem".[3]

Freud certainly condoned Einstein's clear and reasonable views, but his
experience from the First World War had made him pessimistic. In his text on
war and death, he deplores the failure of the western world to develop civilised
ways of solving conflicts of interest. In light of the great progress which had
taken place within technology, the mastery of nature, in the arts and sciences,
one could have expected, writes Freud, to find new solutions concerning
conflicts of interest between nations. Such expectations were, however,
cruelly disappointed.

In accordance with this disillusioned, but also realistic appraisal of humankind's ability to solve conflicts on an international level, Freud's response
to Einstein is a sober judgement of the reality of war, and of humankind's
restricted ability to secure lasting peace.

Freud's tired and uncomfortable tone could also be linked to Einstein's
already having answered the question of the supranational political and legal
initiatives needed to prevent war. Einstein had even ventured into Freud's
domain, and suggested that psychological forces opposing attempts to secure
peace and safety are probably to be found in an intrinsically human hatred and
wish to destroy one's fellow man. However, I think Freud's discomfort in
formulating an answer to the reasons of war is to be found elsewhere, and is,
rather, related to the subject itself, and to the inadequacy of the suggested
explanations. While inviting Freud to join a discussion on the "why" of war,
Einstein had unwittingly touched on a dilemma and a paradox that Freud's
theory at this point had run into. With the dualism between the drives of life
and death, Freud had not only introduced a debatable idea of a drive towards
death, but had also given up the idea of the innate ambiguity of each of the
drives, which could have been an alternative to his ultimate idea of drive
dualism. I shall return to this later. Here, it will suffice to suggest that Freud's
reply to Einstein concerns more and includes matters beyond the possible
reasons for war. Freud had also felt bound to defend his theory of the death
drive. With his invitation, Einstein had precisely asked Freud to share his
knowledge of the depths of the human soul, in order to approach an answer to
what motivates and drives humans to demonstrate the kind of brutality which
is a part of war.

What Einstein in his first letter to Freud referred to as superficial solutions to the securing of peace are far from deserving of being described as
such. These suggestions imply no less than a profound intervention into

national sovereignty and freedom of action. Einstein suggests the setting up of a supranational institution with judicial and legislative authority, to which individual states must cede a part of their sovereignty. Seen in the light of the contemporary situation of nationalistic protectionism, right-wing politics and the threatening collapse of the European Union, Einstein's suggestion appears a beautiful dream from bygone times. Attempts to realise such visions encountered as great obstacles then as now. Powerful psychological forces, continues Einstein, cripple such endeavours, and some of them are not difficult to catch sight of. One such obstacle is the power-hunger of the ruling class of a nation, which refuses every infringement of its sovereignty. Another obstacle is linked to the class that regards war, the production of and trade with arms as an opportunity to attain its own strivings and increase its personal power. The question remains, however, of the nature of the forces which, through propaganda and suggestion, inflame the masses to the point of rage and to sacrifices for a war from which they can only expect suffering and loss. The answer, he suggests, can only lie in a need in humans that drives them to destroy each another. He therefore asks Freud to answer the question of "how to make man proof against the psychosis of hate and destruction".

Freud's answer is dispassionate, wise and sober. By way of introduction, he notes that he can only agree with Einstein's observations, albeit permitting himself to expand on them somewhat. The first half of his reply to Einstein perhaps does not contain any new views, but bears witness of a person who has felt a personal and professional obligation to reflect upon the question of the purpose of war, and on what motivates it. It is important to keep in mind, writes Freud, that power was originally exerted through physical violence, and that the way from might to right went through societies, the cohesion of which could maintain right in opposition to the individual violence. Such societies have always been fragile, since they, from the beginning, have contained different relations – for example, that between men and women, adults and children, rulers and ruled, and as history shows us, there have always existed conflicts of interest and conquests between one society and another, as well as within smaller groups of a single society. However, one cannot equate all wars of conquest. Some of these wars have created large units and a central power, which to a certain extent have limited the eruption of new wars. But not even this endeavour has been able to secure a lasting peace, as it proved difficult to create the necessary cohesion between units gathered through violence.

There are two conditions that bind a given society. Force, with the help of violence, and the emotional ties within the society. These ties occur when groups of individuals create a common ideal and their egos identify with this ideal, and with each other. It is, however, doubtful whether such a socially foundational identification could be created through a common idea, which was the vision behind the founding of the United Nations. Religious and political ideologies have all too clearly revealed themselves as not only insufficient, but they are also seen to exert a pull in the wrong direction in the face of imaginary boundaries and polarised world-views. The cohesion of nations can, to a certain extent, depend upon a conviction of superiority relative to other nations, but this does not prevent internal conflicts of interest and is a fragile and illusory way of maintaining unity. The power of ideas has never effectively replaced real power, concludes Freud, as power has, then and now, relied on violence.

While the first part of Freud's response to Einstein is formulated as the considerations of one reasonable, humanistic and socially critical individual to another, it is the psychoanalyst who is heard in the second part. It is here that the answer to the question on the reasons for war is shown to contain paradoxical statements as well as irresolvable enigmas. Freud continues the letter to Einstein by referring to how he, in his scientific work, has arrived at a theory of the antagonism of human drives. While the so-called life drives strive to preserve and unite humans, the death drive strives towards destruction and, ultimately, death. The opposite tendencies of the drives should not be mistaken for the difference between good and bad. Both drives are necessary for the development of the individual as well as society, and all manifestations of life spring from the dialectic and interplay of the drives. We are thus confronted with the paradox that the drives that want destruction and the death of the other can simultaneously be a constructive aspect of lived life. One here intuits a contradiction between a view insisting on the antagonism of the drives and a view of the drives as inextricably engaged in dialectical interplay.

The concession to the finding that the ego, upon which the survival of the individual depends, is also the object of the sexual drive led Freud to give up his first drive theory, which was based on the opposition between the ego drives and the sexual drives. The two drives were thus shown to be two aspects of the same thing. Freud was reluctant to part with the idea of a fundamental split or conflict within the human psyche and could not reconcile himself with the assumption of drive monism, in other words, the idea of the libido as universal psychic energy. The controversy with Carl Gustav Jung, which eventually led to the end of the relationship was due to this problem, and strengthened Freud's conviction of an antagonism of the drives. This, however, led to some problematic assumptions. The attempt to save the idea of the death drive led him into a biological dead end, and drive dualism came to imply an insurmountable opposition between the life and death drive rather than emphasising the inherent ambiguity of each of the drives.

Beyond the Pleasure Principle, which contains Freud's justification for the introduction of the idea of a death drive, is a complicated text that moves from clinical observations to abstract speculation and naturalistic explanations.[4] In his letter to Einstein, Freud admits that his theory of the death drive has the appearance of a mythology of sorts, but asks, in defence, if it is different in the other sciences. Freud had paved the way to a radical theoretical revision of his drive theory when he gave up the differentiation between sexual drives and ego drives, and a space was thus cleared for an antagonist to that which he gathered under the term "Eros". Experience from clinical work was shown to fill this space. Observations of the phenomenon of repetition pointed to a movement within psychic life which could not be explained on the premise of the human being's quest for pleasure. The concept of repetition was not new, but at this point received new direction and new meaning. As opposed to the repetition of wishes and needs, in the compulsion to repeat it is a question of a need to repeat per se, as when destructive symptoms and patterns of behaviour are repeated without modification, despite their leading only to suffering and pain. Contemporary psychoanalysts have suggested a differentiation between repetition of the same, which is a repetition with variations, and repetition of the identical, which is subject to the repetition compulsion and contains no variation.[5] The repetition compulsion reveals a principle of regulation of mental processes and mechanisms, which reaches beyond the pleasure principle and shows that the human being is not only pleasure-seeking, but is driven by urges that strive towards gratification beyond normal pleasure. Repetition of the identical takes place outside consciousness and memory. The drive is manifested outside the symbolic order and is therefore unreceptive to interpretation or translation from unconscious to conscious. This is a clue to the understanding of phenomena otherwise difficult to understand, such as the symptomatic repercussions of serious trauma, psychosomatic phenomena, anorexic or self-harming behaviour and serious obsessions and depressions. They can all be described as short-circuits of the psychic into the somatic. Or one could say that the repetition compulsion strives to empty and destroy the psychic apparatus with the objective of ridding it of every trace of pain. In the extreme consequence this is synonymous with the breaking down of the ego.

Even something as innocent as a child's endless repetitions of the same game supported the postulate of an extensive compulsion to repeat in the psyche. From the clinical observations of phenomena of repetition, Freud turned to biology to explore if it could demonstrate similar examples of tendencies that counteract development, and on the contrary, bring something once acquired back to an original condition, and possibly bring organic life to an inorganic state. The result of these speculations was the assumption of life emerging under the influence of external forces, and following an incrementally complicated development, ultimately to return to the original state. Simply put, life is a detour on the road to death. This biological anchoring of the death drive gives the impression of a short-circuiting of the attempt to link psychological phenomena of different kinds of repetition with a biologically based theory of the death drive, for how can one equate a child's play with a soldier's repetition of original trauma, and regard both as being manifestations of the death drive?

The final version of drive theory equally banishes the possibility of considering the compulsion to repeat as a fundamental aspect of each drive. There is something daemonic, writes Freud, in the death drive, but he drives out the daemon by grounding it in biology. The daemonic is, precisely, an aspect of the drive's inherent ambiguity. The Slovenian philosopher Mladen Dolar[6] has convincingly argued the inherent duality of the drives. Inherent to the drive is a conservative tendency to return to original situations of gratification, which propels the repetition compulsion, but linked to the drive is also a daemonic disquiet, which is indeed destructive, but also creates possible openings for renewal and guarantees that the drive does not close in on its own circuit, but is, on the contrary, forced out of it. Therefore, concludes Dolar, relying on the assumption of the unifying force of Eros in the face of the destruction of the death drive is of no avail. On the contrary, we should direct our hopes toward the destructive tendency and regard it as a prerequisite for change on the individual as well as the societal or political level. My understanding of this is that the explicitly destructive aspects of the drive's regressive movement, its tendencies towards primitive modes of expression, can be a necessary step for new beginnings.

These abstract ideas resonate with the suggestion of contemporary psychoanalysts that the concept of the death drive needs revision.[7] Instead of speaking of two biological forces, we should differentiate between two distinct principles of psychic regulation. While the first principle binds psychic material and creates psychic representation, the second strives towards destruction and dissolution. The first principle belongs to the sexual life drives, the second to the sexual death drives. It is a fruitful thought, which besides saving the psychoanalytically central concept of the drives, and retaining it on the psychic level, could also shed light on the common observation that love and sexuality also contain aggressive and destructive tendencies. The idea could also help explain why war, among the many torments humans are capable of inflicting on each other, is accompanied by murderous aspects with sexual as well as violent components, and how rape becomes the ultimate humiliation of a fellow human being, serving narcissistic hatred rather than sexual satisfaction.

It was the idea of the death drive that Freud presented to Einstein, and elaborating on this he writes that the human drives take two forms: one, striving to preserve and unite, and another, that strives to destroy and kill. When people are mobilised to war, several motives are in play, all of which point to these two drive tendencies: the noble and banal motives, of which one speaks highly; and the hidden, which are not spoken, but secretly drive their gratifying actions. The death drive manifests itself as aggression and destruction, when it is turned towards the world and others, and in this respect one could say that man preserves his life by destroying other, foreign life. The conclusion must therefore be that the attempt to abolish the aggressive tendencies of the human being is of no avail. At most, one can try to dispel or deflect them, and as far as that goes one must call upon Eros and the emotional ties between fellow men. As if he does not entirely believe in the success of such a project, Freud closes with the following disillusioned statement: "The ideal condition of things would of course be a community of men who had subordinated their instinctual life to the dictatorship of reason. Nothing else could unite men so completely and so tenaciously, even if there were no emotional ties between them. But in all probability that is a Utopian expectation".[8] It is a strange point of view in a man who has devoted his entire professional life to examine the powers opposing the dictates of reason, and who has not only recognised but also praised them. I read this statement in light of the dualism that the introduction of the death drive entailed, and which here is manifested as the opposition between reason and the drives. But is reason, which we ascribe to the ego, not also the locus of aggression and repression, besides being indissolubly tied to rationalisation, eager to deliver good reasons serving to conceal evil intent?

The idea of the dictatorship of reason as Utopian hope would, some few years later, manifest itself with such massive and terrifying reality that following generations were compelled to think deeper and wider on the question of the why of war. Einstein has said that with the development of atomic power everything has changed, except our thinking. I will allow myself to understand it thus; thinking, despite its excellent achievements, also comprises primitive forms. Under certain conditions, thinking can regress, and we then witness primitive forms of thinking characterised by projection, denial and splitting. There is an implicit danger and illusion in the belief that the existence of atomic weapons would suffice to secure world peace.[9] Such equilibrium in a system of mutual fear has an inherent fragility. Fear begets hate, and hate leads to new forms of fear, and worst of all, this vicious cycle creates a primitive form of thinking marked by projective defences. This variant of thinking is to be found in psychotic ideation, where the difference between reality and fantasy breaks down, and paranoid thinking risks being elevated to the status of true reality. When a person projects his/her aggression into another, the latter can be perceived as the very reflection of evil, and it then is not a question of downright projection but of belief that calls for action, and in such a universe of projective omnipotence, action runs the risk of being lethal. We witnessed this when former American President George W. Bush introduced the term "axis of evil" and made Saddam Hussein the image of this evil, in the same movement legitimising necessary sanctions against the latter. We see it today when people intrepidly blow themselves to pieces in service of a higher cause, in the belief of a reward in the afterworld, thus probably finding an outlet for hatred of the present world, which for them has been foreign, inaccessible and hostile.

Knowing that total destruction is a possibility has altered our relation to death. Seen in this perspective, death is no longer the natural ending of life, nor the unwillingly accepted outcome of conventional war. The prospect of dying in an atomic war creates inexplicable emptiness and nameless dread. The same could be said of the terror which today illustrates the conversion into action of pure hate, under the aegis of religious fanaticism.

Experiences from Auschwitz compelled a number of European critical thinkers, such as Hannah Arendt and Theodor W. Adorno, to formulate entirely new questions and create new perspectives on the relation between the development of civilisation and the morality and thinking of the individual. In her report on the Eichmann trial, Arendt introduced the term "banality of evil".[10] The problem with Eichmann was that he gave the impression of being an ordinary person. He was neither perverse nor sadistic, but terribly and terrifyingly normal. His actions were not the result of conscious evil, but of blind obedience, or as Adorno put it: "Triviality is evil – triviality, that is, in the form of consciousness and mind that adapts itself to the world as it is, which obeys the principle of inertia".[11] Like Adorno, Arendt differentiated between banal and radical evil. Radical evil is the evil deed, cruelty which is blind to the other's suffering, and that resists every attempt at understanding. It is the kind of face-to-face evil known in traditional warfare and from the genocides and mass killings of which we have been witness in Bosnia, and lately, in Syria. In the case of Eichmann, Arendt observed a new form of evil, which had profound consequences for her work on thinking and morality.

This new form of evil could not be traced to some evil character trait or pathology, nor to ideological conviction in its practitioner, but to something as seemingly banal as lacking the capacity to think. In consequence of this observation, she asked if there was a link between this deficient ability for thought and what we normally call conscience, and she suggested that they were two sides of the same thing. Conscience is a form of afterthought, through which we stop to examine our thoughts and actions. Conscience manifests itself as afterthought. It is a thought that wakes after we have committed or fantasised a guilty act which is irreconcilable with the morality we subscribe to. Thinking means that we regard ourselves, and it shows that the self – in Søren Kierkegaard's words – is a relation that relates to itself. In this relation, or split of the self, lies the possibility and obligation of morality. When judgement is impaired, man's actions become morally blind, and this occurs, according to Arendt, under totalitarian regimes. I would like to add that moral blindness is always a risk when people let themselves be governed by a given set of mores without asking whether these mores are morally acceptable. Eichmann's refraining from thinking and the exercise of judgement was not least due to his projection of his ego ideal onto "the leader", whom he hereafter blindly obeyed, but – it is to be noted – not without selfishly securing certain privileges such as promotions, among other things. Transferred to the present, Arendt's concept of banal evil can throw light on the absence of self-reflection and moral awareness that can be noted in the dominance of technological and bureaucratic reason that have become characteristic of modern civilisation.

Contemporary scholar of modernity Zygmunt Bauman has taken up Arendt's thinking and effected a thorough and critical analysis of the Holocaust with the objective of pointing out the afore-mentioned problem of modern civilisation.[12] Like Arendt, he points out that not only Eichmann, but all "ingredients" of the Holocaust are well known from everything we recognise as modernity – its spiritual goals, its priorities and its immanent view of the world. There is no major difference between today's mass production with its vision of universal material abundance and the technology that was used in the concentration camps and their vision of excessive death, writes Bauman. Structurally, the machinery of destruction does not differ much from the totality of well-organised German society, and even if modernity was not the cause of the Holocaust, it was a necessary condition, Bauman continues. Excepting gigantic moral decline, there is not much that separates the bureaucracy of the concentration camps from modern, rational bureaucracy with its formally and morally blind demands of efficiency. The loss of moral judgement, on which Arendt speculated in the case of Eichmann, has three prerequisites on the societal level, writes Bauman. Violence was authorised. That is to say, orders were issued from legally elected units. Actions were subordinated to standard routines, and finally, extensive dehumanisation took place. Bauman has illustrated dehumanisation with the expression "universe of obligations", which defines the group to which we feel obligated. Outside of this group, there is no obligation. The exclusion of the Jews from German society was tantamount to excluding them from the universe of obligations. This idea is no less relevant today, when the problematic of refugees and migrants tends to create clear demarcations between groups that fall within the universe of obligations and others that do not.

In his description of mass psychology, Freud touched upon the aforementioned question of the loss of moral judgement. When individual members of a mass identify their leader as a common ego ideal, they give up their own ego ideal and willingly surrender to the common ideal. Hereby individual moral judgement is transferred to the leader and is replaced by moral feeling, creating obedience to the point of complete submission. This kind of obedience could throw light on the case of Eichmann.

Eichmann was not a sadist – at least not in the usual sense. One could, however, with French psychoanalyst Jacques Lacan's definition of "sadism", which says that the sadist puts himself at the service of the other's enjoyment, call Eichmann a sadist.[13] His crime therefore lay not only in his failure to think, but in having made himself an instrument for the enjoyment of the other. In other words, Eichmann offered himself as the vessel for the other's sadistic and hateful pleasure. The same could be said to be the case in the shot that kills. The source of the drive that results in the lethal shot is not necessarily to be found in the person who fires it. The source of the hate and hostility is to be found elsewhere. The responsibility of the messenger lies in his having put himself at the service of the effectuation of the message's goal.

Neither Arendt nor Bauman were particularly interested in psychoanalysis, but to my mind, their critical and valuable thoughts deserve to be complemented with the concepts of psychoanalysis, which add a dimension to their philosophical and sociological analyses.

When Arendt says of Eichmann that his crime lay in failing to think and make moral judgements, it is close at hand to ask if more was not at stake. Even if the evil was banal, it was nevertheless a question of evil. In the brief text *Negation,*[14] Freud demonstrated a defence mechanism that could elaborate the concept of banal evil and show how widely-spread and common it is. This refined mechanism consists in something repressed, or something of which one does not want to think, getting access to consciousness on the proviso that it is negated. There is intellectual acceptance of the repressed, and simultaneously the essence of repression is preserved. To be added is the important assumption that negation belongs to the death drive, whereas affirmation, conversely, belongs to the life drive or Eros. In my experience, negation is a common defence mechanism in severely narcissistically disturbed people. They are on the one hand capable, at no personal cost, so to speak, to acknowledge drive impulses and wishes, only to negate their significance. Not least, these concessions take place at the cost of accompanying affects such as shame and guilt, which are isolated and remain repressed behind intellectual acceptance. These people relate to the unconscious with a kind of arrogant cynicism. Negation is not restricted to psychopathology. In an article on the lie in political rhetoric, I have discussed this defence mechanism in light of Jean-Paul Sartre's concept "bad faith", which could aptly be added to Arendt's and Bauman's analyses of moral decline in the individual and in society.[15]

As opposed to the simple lie, bad faith is a lie turned toward the subject itself, and it adds an element of self-deception to the simple lie, which is turned toward the other. In bad faith, the liar and the one lied to are one and the same. In order to lie to himself, the person needs to know the truth, but at the moment it becomes possible to hide this truth, it no longer exists, and the person can convince himself and others that he/she is acting in good faith. Bad faith is not something one consciously chooses. Bad faith, writes Sartre, is something one falls into, as one falls asleep.[16]

Through the years, we have been witnesses to lies becoming a rhetorical figure in politics. The displacement from rhetorical persuasion to statements against better knowledge, however, received its most salient expression in connection with the Iraq War, where in several quarters it was claimed that the alleged existence of weapons of mass destruction was not something one believed, but something one knew. When the lie is no longer a rhetorical trope, but approaches bad faith, there is a decline in public morals, and one disturbing aspect of such decline is that it is not sanctioned. There exist numerous examples of lies becoming part of the political rhetoric. Particularly scandalous, of course, is when lies or bad faith conceal the truth of the reason for war. When the lie becomes bad faith, we are faced with a kind of fraud bypassing afterthought and evading sanctions, which is particularly serious for general morality, when it is displayed on the political scene.

Freud and Einstein did not have the experiences that Auschwitz brought, but through their reasonable discussion, they showed their commitment to examine and formulate critical questions on the subject of war and every war's catastrophic consequences for the individual and for culture. I would like to maintain that their correspondence could be read like the "petition principii" that Max Horkheimer and Theodor W. Adorno formulated one year after the end of World War II. In *Dialectic of Enlightenment,* they write that even if we acclaim enlightened thinking as the freedom of a society, we must consider the regressive aspect with which this thinking is interwoven.[17] To my mind, it is this deliberation that Freud and Einstein undertook, at a point some few years preceding the Second World War. Wholly in the spirit of Horkheimer and Adorno, Freud closes his letter to Einstein with the question if we must necessarily condemn war, and he answers that we must, because we are civilised human beings. The civilisation that contains the prerequisites of devastation is, in other words, the very same which urges us to condemn devastation.

Notes

1 Freud, S. (1933 [1932]). Why War? *The Standard Edition of the Psychological Works of Sigmund Freud,* Vol. XXII. London: The Hogarth Press.
2 Freud, S. (1915). Thoughts for the Times on War and Death. *The Standard Edition of the Psychological Works of Sigmund Freud,* Vol. XIV. London: The Hogarth Press.
3 Freud, S. (1933 [1932]). Why War? *The Standard Edition of the Psychological Works of Sigmund Freud,* Vol. XXII, p. 199. London: The Hogarth Press.
4 Freud, S. (1920). Beyond the Pleasure Principle. *The Standard Edition of the Psychological Works of Sigmund Freud,* Vol. XVIII. London: The Hogarth Press.
5 See de M'uzan, M. (2013). *Death and Identity. Being and the Psycho-Sexual Drama.* London: Karnac.
6 Dolar, M. (2017). Of Drives and Culture. *Problemi International. Society for Theoretical Psychoanalysis* 1(1):55–79.
7 See Laplanche, J. (2011). *Freud and the Sexual.* New York: International Psychoanalytic Books; Green, A. (2001). *Life Narcissism, Death Narcissism.* London: Free Association Books.
8 Freud, S. (1933 [1932]). Why War? *The Standard Edition of the Psychological Works of Sigmund Freud,* Vol. XXII, p. 213. London: The Hogarth Press.
9 See Segal, H. (1997). *Psychoanalysis, Literature and War.* London: Routledge.
10 Arendt, H. (1964). *Eichmann in Jerusalem. A Report on the Banality of Evil.* London: Penguin Books.
11 Adorno, T.W. (1998/2000). *Metaphysics: Concepts and Problems,* p. 115. Stanford, California: Stanford University Press.
12 Bauman, Z. (1989). *Modernity and Holocaust.* New York: Cornell University Press.
13 Lacan, J. (1966/2006). Kant with Sade. In: *Écrits,* pp. 645–671. New York: W. W. Norton & Company.
14 Freud, S. (1925). Negation. *The Standard Edition of the Psychological Works of Sigmund Freud,* Vol. XIX. London: The Hogarth Press.
15 Gammelgaard, J. (2013). Demokratiets arbejdsplads. Om løgnen som politisk retorik på Christiansborg. In: N.M.C. Nickelsen (eds.) *Arbejdslivets Skyggesider.* Aarhus: Klim.
16 Sartre, J.-P. (1943/1992). *Being and Nothingness. A Phenomenological Essay on Ontology,* p. 89. Translated by H.E. Barnes. New York: Simon & Schuster.
17 Horkheimer, M., & Adorno, T.W. (1944/2002). *The Dialectic of Enlightenment.* Stanford, California: Stanford University Press.

Chapter 8

Questioning civilization

In his text from 1908 on culturally constructed sexual mores and their relationship to nervous illness, Freud gave a first extensive account of his view of the relation between the life of the drives of the individual and civilisation, or culture.[1] In accordance with German tradition, Freud did not differentiate between the afore-mentioned terms. This implied that he was unable to utilise the difference to observe the opposition between civilisation and culture that other critics of civilisation had noted.[2] Conversely, Freud was not blind to the inverse relation between the individual and civilisation. His main thesis was that civilisation necessitates drive renunciation. Man must, in other words, pay a price in the form of loss of pleasure and happiness for the security offered by civilisation. For some, this price can be so high as to make them enemies of civilisation – a view that can be tracked back to his earliest writings and which culminates in *Civilization and its Discontents* from 1930.[3]

In the 1908 text, civilisation is depicted as a forbidding and pleasure-inhibiting instance. Culturally created demands and requirements curb and impede man's pleasure-seeking activities. Freud was able to observe the result of pervasive drive renunciation in the neurotics who turned to him with inexplicable and painful symptoms. The neuroses clearly spoke of an unsatisfied sexual life. In a brief historical sketch, Freud hypothesised the genesis of bourgeois society's sexual repression: Early in the development of civilisation, sexual expression reigned relatively free, as humans were unconcerned with reproduction. Hereafter followed a stage when sexuality was restricted to serve reproduction, followed by a phase when only legitimate reproduction, that is to say, reproduction within the confines of marriage, was accepted. Freud's criticism of civilisation should be seen against the background of the massive repression of sexual pleasure that he observed in his patients. But it should equally be understood in light of the concept of the sexual drive that his clinical observations necessitated.

When Freud introduced the concept of the drive, he did not as yet know what a drive was, and even less, what a sexual drive was. However, he gathered his experience from clinical work and systematised his ideas on the sexual drive in the epochal 1905[4] work on the theory of sexuality. Here, he thoroughly challenges two dogmas observed in the common understanding of sexuality. The first dogma claims that sexuality appears along with the sexual maturation of puberty. The second limits sexuality to what we understand as genital sexuality. The sexually mature individual's genital pleasure is, however, the end-product of lengthy development. Early on, the child finds its way to pleasurable experiences, emerging from the body as a whole. Infantile poly-morphous sexuality is the concept for the pleasure connected with the child's body, and not least, the body's orifices. As opposed to that of the adult, the child's sexual pleasure has no culmination. The child does not experience anything like orgasm. The child is sensual and experiences a pleasure that is best described as sustained fore-pleasure. Even if infantile sexuality lives its own hidden life throughout the years of childhood, it does not disappear, neither do the accompanying unconscious fantasies. This creates a problem when the child reaches maturation at puberty. The place that the young person's sexuality is to take is already occupied by the traces left by the early sensations of pleasure and, not least, by the fantasies these have left behind. With sexual maturation, the young person is faced with the task of sub-ordinating infantile pleasure to the sexuality that brings people together in genital pleasure-seeking.

Neurotic sexual inhibition is brought about when original, polymorphous sexual pleasure is subjugated to genital sexuality. This restriction does not always occur, as manifested in the perversions, among other things. Here, the pleasure which is repressed in the neuroses is manifest, so that the perversions can be said to relate to the neuroses as positive to negative. The pervert is, in other words, fixated in an infantile form of pleasure, which has not been integrated during personal development. It is a pleasure that strives towards nothing besides its gratification and is therefore oblivious of the person to whom the pleasure seems to be directed.

For most normal people in Freud's time, it was a question of inhibited and restricted sexual life, created by drive-denying sexual mores. There is, how-ever, a limit to the extent to which people are able to adhere to the rules of culture, and the mores that dominated in the bourgeoisie of Victorian Vienna had some unhappy consequences for marital life. This was, of course, parti-cularly relevant for the wives, who often became overly delicate and moral, as opposed to the husbands, who perhaps evaded neurosis, but led a double life in relation to ruling sexual morality. Freud's experience had taught him that sexual abstinence not only creates frustration, but that human sexual life has importance for character formation. Inhibited sexuality created people who lacked initiative and manifested inhibition in their general life-style, while others developed early fixations, resulting in aberrant or perverse sexual be-haviour. When the drives are repressed, and fixated as a consequence of the development of civilisation, "fantasy will go to the dogs", as Max Horkheimer and Theodor W. Adorno expressed it.[5] In other words, fantasies linked to sexual life become stereotypical and rigid. Freud expressed it thus: Repression of sexuality leads to the restriction of development and a lack of creative curiosity. He concludes his criticism of civilised morality by asking if the sacrifices demanded by civilisation are worth it, and if people do not have the right to a modicum of happiness and pleasure as compensation for the abstinence imposed by culture.

While Freud, as previously mentioned, in his early writings saw an opposition between the individual and civilisation, his outlook in *Civilization and its Discontents* – particularly towards the end – is more dialectic, in the sense of Horkheimer and Adorno. *Civilization and its Discontents* could be read as an anticipation of Horkheimer and Adorno's *The Dialectic of Enlightenment*, written in 1944, in reaction to Hitler's regime with its destruction and terror. Their work is a long, thorough critique of civilisation and a protest against the horrors people are prepared to inflict on each another. But while the founders of the Frankfurt school remain on an abstract, philosophical level, from which they reveal their disillusioned view of the world, refraining from instructions on how to concretely apply their criticism, Freud's text is much closer to reality, at some points bordering on common knowledge. He was fully aware of this and thus admits: "In none of my previous writings have I had so strong a feeling as now that what I am describing is common knowledge, and that I am using up paper and ink, and, in due course, the compositor's and printer's work and material in order to expound things which are, in fact, self-evident".[6] Freud is probably thinking of the description of the basic features of civilisation, which indeed do not present much novelty. Culture, writes Freud, first and foremost consists in the mastery of nature, which humans have accomplished with the help of technology and science. To culture, however, belong certain absolutely unnecessary things, so-called "cultural goods", to which art, not least, belongs, but also ideas, ideals and spirituality in the broad sense. To be added to the list of the characteristics of culture is cleanliness, hygiene and the urge towards order. The regulation of human communities, as it occurs within the family, in social groupings and in society as the overarching frame of these communities, also belong to culture, and it is precisely here that the crux is located. It is in the regulation of human relations that culture encounters its most serious obstacles, and here progress degenerates into decline and barbarism.

Freud is as disillusioned as Horkheimer and Adorno, in the works of which pessimism and resignation are obvious. Every progress bears its own downfall, they write. Not because progress fails. Ironically, successful progress contains its own opposite, their point being that continuous progress leads to continuous decline.[7]

Freud's culture-critical writings decidedly involve a certain pessimism, but it would be more appropriate to speak of a sober realism springing from the insight that we humans are incapable of preventing the suffering we have imposed upon ourselves and on others. However, Freud also speaks in gentler terms. The most compelling passages in *Civilization and its Discontents* are those where Freud speaks as a human being, without reference to his theory, when he enumerates the means we all use to alleviate our suffering. These, however, are all seriously limited and cannot compare with direct drive gratification, writes Freud, with bitter realism.

Freud's critique of enlightened civilisation is as pitiless as that of Adorno and Horkheimer. Since our human communities are the source of culture or ci-vilisation, we touch on the paradox contained in the title of Freud's essay, namely that the main culprit of our misery is "our so-called culture". That is to say that the major reason for our unhappiness is the same as that which has made us cultural beings.

Towards the end of *Civilization and its Discontents*, however, the analysis of the relationship between culture and the individual takes a turn which is to reveal an originality and complexity that make the final part of the essay far more disturbing than the first. Here, the relationship between the drives of the individual and culture's limited capacity to compensate for the renunciations required is seen in a completely new perspective. Approaching the question whether cultural development coincides with individual development, Freud introduces, inspired by Charles Darwin, a story in mythical form. Originally, humans were organised as a primal horde led by a despotic ruler, who kept the women to himself and expelled the maturing sons from the horde. One day, however, the exiled sons came together, murdered and ate the father. The consumption of the father was an act of identification, by which the sons took part of the father's strength. What the father had previously forbidden the sons, they now forbade themselves. They created a symbol for the father, or father-substitute, and tried to undo their deed by declaring a prohibition against murder of the paternal substitute. This was the birth of totemism. The sons refrained from enjoying the fruit of their crime by imposing abstinence on themselves in relation to the now-freed women. Thus, arose another aspect of human culture: the norm of exogamy and the prohibition of incest.

How are we to understand this story? It is important not to misunderstand it as a causal and historical explanation of the creation of culture, but rather to see it as an image, serving to visualise the relation between the individual and cultural development. With his fable, Freud wished to understand the meaning and implications of life as cultural beings. From clinical experience, he learned that neurotic symptoms conceal ambivalent feelings towards the parents, who are both loved and hated. The ambivalence leads to guilt, and the symptom could be understood as a symbolical act of atonement. The same pattern is to be found in the forces that determine the development of culture. The relationship to people outside the family is equally ambivalent. We harbour both love and hate for our fellow humans. Emotional ambivalence leads to guilt, and guilt – being one of the most unbearable emotions a human being can have – leads to the need for reparation on the individual as well as societal level.

Freud could have limited himself to suggest that neurosis and culture are related in one way or another, instead of using a story that appears rather fantastical. But the mere stating of a relation between neurosis and culture does not say much about how this relation comes to be and results in a form of circularity. Freud needed a third term, in the form of an image or fable, to show the interconnectedness of neurosis and culture, and therefore invented or found the story of the primal horde and parricide. By telling a story instead of using more stringent, conceptual language, he was able to visualise culture as the result of ambivalence, guilt and atonement. Freud's use of mythical material as illustrations of the ideas he was processing is legendary.

We find the same use of mythological material in *Dialectic of Enlightenment*, when Horkheimer and Adorno praise pre-philosophical, mythical consciousness. One of the most fascinating chapters in the book treats Homer's epic on Odysseus as the emblem of an early form of enlightenment, created at a time when the world was not yet "disenchanted", as Max Weber so poignantly put it.[8] Myth has its justification as a corrective to theoretical reason, as it strives to open layers of signification where conceptual language falls short. Freud's frequent use of mythical material should be seen as an attempt to colour language with that which cannot be said, but nevertheless intrudes and insists on being expressed.

Through the figurative, mythical rendition of the relationship between the individual and culture, an aspect of the super-ego was clearly manifested, which would not have been possible in the study of the individual. The superego was, from this point, the instance of the individual that answers to the law, that is to say, the lawful regulation of social life, as Slavoj Žižek has expressed it. This could be illustrated by two culturally created biblical commandments and prohibitions, both appealing to the super-ego, but which are mute as to the drive renunciations that result from compliance to them: "Thou shalt love thy neighbour as thyself" and "Thou shalt not kill". The first of these is an absurdity, writes Freud, as it is not possible to love the other as oneself. It is, besides, a mockery of love. A love that does not choose loses its worth, he claims. There exists, and will probably always exist, a quantum of antagonism between love and culture. Only in principle can one imagine a culture where people are libidinally sated within themselves, or in other words, resting in sound narcissistic equilibrium besides being interconnected in a working community. To this is to be added that behind the commandment of loving the other as oneself stands a piece of reality which is readily denied. Man is not a gentle, love-seeking creature, at most able to defend himself when attacked. A good share of aggressive tendencies makes up the drives we are equipped with. This fact can explain why culture has found it necessary to prohibit killing. If this tendency was not alive within us, the prohibition would have been redundant. Abstinence from natural destructive tendencies strengthens the internal restraint already created by sexual renunciation, and a closer inspection of man's destructive tendencies will be shown to contain an enigmatic and uncanny mechanism in the entire problem complex we refer to as morality.

Cultural development rests on the turning inwards of aggression. It is introjected, as technical language puts it. It is, so to speak, expelled back to where it came from and directed towards the self. The super-ego, through the voice of conscience, directs aggression that would have been turned against others back to the self. The super-ego is, in other words, the aspect of the subject which demands drive renunciation as well as equipping us with guilt. The super-ego, and conscience, emerge relatively late in human development. The young child does not discriminate good from bad, and learns to differentiate good behaviour from bad through the parent's praise and punishment. For the child, bad is what is punished by the loss of the parent's love, this being the most severe punishment for a child, and it is out of anxiety for this loss that the child learns to refrain from actions which could threaten it with the loss of love. It is not yet a question of conscience, but of anxiety connected to loss of love. Neither is it an early form of guilt that drives the child to abstain bad actions, but only the intention to evade consequent punishment. What we call moral decay consists in part of regression to this infantile form of guilt.

Generally, this changes when authority becomes an internal matter, through the establishment of the super-ego. Only hereafter is it relevant to speak of the voice of conscience. The implementation of the super-ego and conscience eradicate the difference between bad actions and the thought of committing them. Nothing escapes the eye of the super-ego. In other words, guilt can take two forms. It can either be a reaction to the punishment of authority or the expression of the super-ego's repudiation. The first entails abstinence from drive gratification, while the second leads to a need for punishment. In other words, there is a link between drive abstinence and guilt feelings, and this link is validated by the fact that it is precisely the renunciation of drive gratification that equips the super-ego with the aggression that is directed against the self. The circle is closed, and we can observe that while guilt was originally the cause of renunciation, this is later reversed, with the effect that renunciation becomes the source of the super-ego's punishment. Every new renunciation increases the super-ego's severity and intolerance. Each time we refrain from directing our aggression outwards, to the world and its objects, it is taken over by the super-ego, which in turn directs it against the ego. The severity of the super-ego is not proportionate to the severity of the authority to which we were once subjected, but to the magnitude of the aggression which could not be directed towards authority, and is instead turned inwards and directed against the ego. In this way, the ego is afflicted with guilt. This is to say that guilt is anger which is not directed against the other, making guilt the most important part of the discontent that man pays in order to be a part of culture. Even if it might sound absurd, anger is frequently a vent for unbearable guilt. Guilt and anger can therefore result in the spiralling of violence.

However, culture disposes of another means to neutralise human aggressive tendencies. Love has its share in cultural life, in the sense that it is one of the most important means at the disposal of civilisation when it summons Eros as a shield against the human destructive tendencies. One of the tasks of culture is to bind humans in communities, firstly in the family and later in collective and social communities. These bonds, however, are not exclusively loving. All human social links are ambivalent, coloured by loving as well as hostile feelings which lead to guilt, and since culture presupposes a necessary shift from the family to the groupings of society, guilt is inextricably tied to cultural development. The price for cultural development, Freud concludes, is paid with the loss of happiness which is a consequence of guilt.

It is thought-provoking that Freud's theory of the Oedipus complex, based on paternal authority, came into being at a time when this authority was about to lose its power and influence. The question is whether Freud's analysis of culture is meaningful today, when authority has received a new significance beyond the patriarchal configuration it still had on the threshold of modernity. With the loss of paternal authority one can assume that the super-ego assumes a new and different structuring and economical position. Zygmunt Bauman[9] introduced the term "liquid modernity" to denote the transition to a new form of capitalism – a light one, as opposed to the powerful capitalism that dates back to the birth of modern industrialism. The concept of liquid modernity connotes not only general economics, but a way of life dependent on mobility, flexibility, outsourcing and, on the psychological level, insecurity, indeterminacy and fragility. There are no leaders who tell us what to do, thus freeing the individual from responsibility. There are, at most, advisors, and one of the major differences between leaders and advisors is that while the former are to be followed, the latter are hired and possibly fired. The conditions of existence in liquid modernity and consequently consumerism entail that a traditional virtue such as the postponement of gratification is no longer acknowledged as such. On the contrary, it is stripped of its ethical and protective function and replaced by the demand for immediate fulfilment. One could expect that liquid modernity would manifest itself in another, or at least other, aspects of the super-ego, which in Freud's time emerged under patriarchally determined authority. With his concept of the obscene superego, Žižek[10] suggests an answer that complements Bauman's social analysis.

Žižek expands Freud's assumption of the link between drive abstinence and guilt by adding that the super-ego has a dark side, deriving an obscene enjoyment, and that this illegal enjoyment is an answer to the lack in the official law, or the official moral code. Since the law is never all-encompassing, and therefore cannot stand as guarantee for all moral regulation, it is necessarily complemented by unwritten laws and rituals, which function as safety vents for the discharge of drive impulses that are not officially permitted. Such organised, ritualised and cleansing forms of affective discharge have their prototype in classical Greek tragedy, which was taken over by the carnivals and festivals of today. Within the setting of a ritualised scene, and protected by an aesthetic illusion, the antagonistic forces of society can find expression and offer an accepted form of discharge of drive pressures that are normally held in check by the prohibitions of the internalised super-ego.

In traditional societies, statutory rules could be sidelined within the boundaries of ritualised festivals, but with the ideology of equality inherent to modernity, and the institution of liquid authority, the patriarchal determination of official and collective spaces disappears, and at this point the relation between official law and the obscene superego undergoes a radical alteration, writes Žižek. Where earlier were tragedy and carnival, today debauchery takes the form of the enjoyment that Jacques Lacan has termed "jouissance", an enjoyment beyond the pleasure principle and therefore an absolute pleasure without bounds. Enjoyment at any price. Žižek points out that this aspect of the super-ego is not represented in official discourse, as it is not available as recorded text. The side of the super-ego that is lived out as the return of the repressed, in the form of excessive enjoyment, seen in mass rape or on a larger scale in acts of terrorism, originates in an internal voice which, like a stranger, intrudes and disrupts the internal equilibrium of the individual or group. In accordance with Freud's analysis of the discontents of civilisation, Žižek understands the obscene aspect of the super-ego as the expression of collective guilt or, more precisely, as the fetishistic denial of this guilt. One example could be the communist who, in the Soviet Union of the 1930s claimed that the communist rule consisted of a group of terrorists, that thousands of people were persecuted and shot without proof, only to be told that he had not understood that what was happening, on the contrary, was a means to a higher end in the form of class-less solidarity. It could be argued that all forms of blind obedience to a community are inherently fetishistic, serving to repudiate a truth that is not to be revealed. One such lie is manifested in the former American President Donald Trump's revitalisation of the American dream, packaged in the rhetoric of making America great again. Andersen's tale *The Emperor's New Clothes* could be a fitting image of a common lie being more effective in binding a group than the truth. Guilt manifests itself not only as the perverse reverse side of the super-ego, but is found as a non-pathological disturbance in us all, thus confirming Freud's analysis of guilt as an essential condition for civilised man. Authors and philosophers have made the same observation.

The paradoxical nature of guilt is central to the works of Franz Kafka. The protagonist of *The Trial*, Josef K, a respected and conscientious citizen, is captured within an opaque judicial apparatus, the ramifications of which eventually ensnare his every movement. In his blind and powerless struggle against what appears a primitive, not to say infantile, logic, he capitulates and assumes the guilt that he will come to experience as his own. The gaze of the other, condensed in a sterile and obscene superego, closes all roads of escape.

We experience this indeterminate guilt when confronted with representatives of the law and register a suggestion of guilt disregarding the clarity of our conscience. There is a link between this abstract guilt and our ignorance of it. Our ignorance comes from a different, strange place. Martin Heidegger has introduced the beautiful metaphor on the voice of conscience not speaking directly, but occupying a silent background, nevertheless possessing imperativity, thus forcing us to soberly consider what we should do.

The philosophers do not speak of a super-ego. It is a psychoanalytical term, a structural concept that demonstrates how guilt appears and develops within the individual. With its explanation, psychoanalysis seeks to show how, within the "innocent" child, develops an internal contradiction between the drives, the ego, and the super-ego. The super-ego is simultaneously the harsh master the ego must obey, a punitive instance and an instance equipped with an obscene aspect capable of abusing the gaps in official law in order to sanction primitive drive discharge within the bounds of unofficial, unwritten law and morality. Seen in this light, it is not strange that Freud, and others with him, took a critical stance to the human trait that some have too much, others too little of. In one of his last lectures, Freud refers to Immanuel Kant, who, in his *Critique of Practical Reason,* said that there are two things that constantly fill the mind with new awe and wonder, the more often and the longer we reflect on them: "The starry heavens above me and the moral law within me". Freud comments thus: "a pious man might well be tempted to honour these two things as the masterpieces of creation. The stars are indeed magnificent, but as regards conscience God has done an uneven and careless piece of work".[11]

Against the background of this soberly realistic verdict, it is noteworthy that Freud, in a brief and overlooked text, expresses another stance, closer to that of Kant. More than twenty years after the publication of his essay on jokes, in 1927 Freud wrote a small essay on humour.[12] The effect of the joke as well as of humour is due to the release of feelings through laughter. Both jokes and humour permit a temporary lowering of the repression barrier. They are, however, qualitatively different, as humour is more sophisticated than the joke. Neither does a humoristic association result in the kind of laughter that the joke spontaneously releases. Humour rather brings about a complicit smile. The essence of humour is a trait in the humoristic individual more than in the individual that witnesses it. This differentiates humour from the joke, the effect of which depends on somebody laughing. Humour concerns an individual's relation to him/herself. The knowing, sophisticated quality that characterises humour is, at first sight, the expression of the ego's narcissism, a claim of sovereignty and invulnerability in the face of the harshness and contingency of reality. In humour a subject elevates him/herself, like the parents over the child, when they smile at its childish sorrows and worries. It is to be added that children with a sense of humour can take the same position and exhibit a maturity far beyond their actual age. Even if the brief essay on humour does not claim to be comprehensive, it points in the direction of finding the essence of humour in the relation between the ego and the super-ego.

In his exploration of the joke, Freud suggests that the joke is an addition from the unconscious that gives the joke its effect and makes us laugh. In the same way it could be said of humour, that it receives its comical effect though an addition from the super-ego. Laughter entails the easing of repression; unconscious impulses are freed and create a comical effect. Humour entails a temporary lightening of the severity of the super-ego, which has a freeing effect on the ego.

The most interesting aspect of this account is the completely new function that is given to the super-ego, which we usually associate with severe drive abstinence. Here, however, we see how the superego permits the ego a modicum of pleasure or joy. The crucial point is that the ego enters a relation to itself, putting itself on par with the super-ego, thus giving the ego a sense of being better than itself. The ego takes the place of the super-ego, and from this elevated position it takes a humoristic view of its own daily activities and strivings. Humour thus bears witness of a subject's maturity, and is one of the most powerful weapons against the discontent created from the drive re-nunciation that culture imposes on us.

Notes

1 Freud, S. (1908). "Civilized" sexual morality and modern nervous illness. *The Standard Edition of the Complete Psychological Works of Sigmund Freud*, Vol. IX. London: The Hogarth Press.
2 When the famous Polish film director Krysztof Kieślowski in 1994 received the Sonning award (translator's note: Danish film award), he claimed, in his speech, that civilisation is what destroys culture.
3 Freud, S. (1930). Civilization and its Discontents. *The Standard Edition of the Complete Psychological Works of Sigmund Freud*, Vol. XXI. London: The Hogarth Press.
4 Freud, S. (1905). Three Essays on the Theory of Sexuality. *The Standard Edition of the Complete Psychological Works of Sigmund Freud*, Vol. VII. London: The Hogarth Press.
5 Horkheimer, M., & Adorno, T.W. (1944/2002). *The Dialectic of Enlightenment*. Stanford, California: Stanford University Press.
6 Freud, S. (1930). Civilization and its Discontents. *The Standard Edition of the Complete Psychological Works of Sigmund Freud*, p. 117, Vol. XXI. London: The Hogarth Press.
7 Horkheimer, M., & Adorno, T.W. (1944/2002). *The Dialectic of Enlightenment*. Stanford, California: Stanford University Press.
8 Weber, M. (1930/2010). *The Protestant Ethic and the Spirit of Capitalism*. Eastford, Connecticut, Martino Fine Books.
9 Bauman, Z. (2000). *Liquid Modernity*. Cambridge: Polity Press.
10 Žižek, S. (1994). *The Metastases of Enjoyment. On women and causality*. Memphis: Verso.
11 Freud, S. (1933[1932]). New introductory lectures on psycho-analysis, XXXI: Dissection of the personality. *The Standard Edition of the Complete Psychological Works of Sigmund Freud*, Vol. XXII, p. 61. London: The Hogarth Press.
12 Freud, S. (1927). Humour. *The Standard Edition of the Complete Psychological Works of Sigmund Freud*, Vol. XXI, pp. 159–167. London: The Hogarth Press.

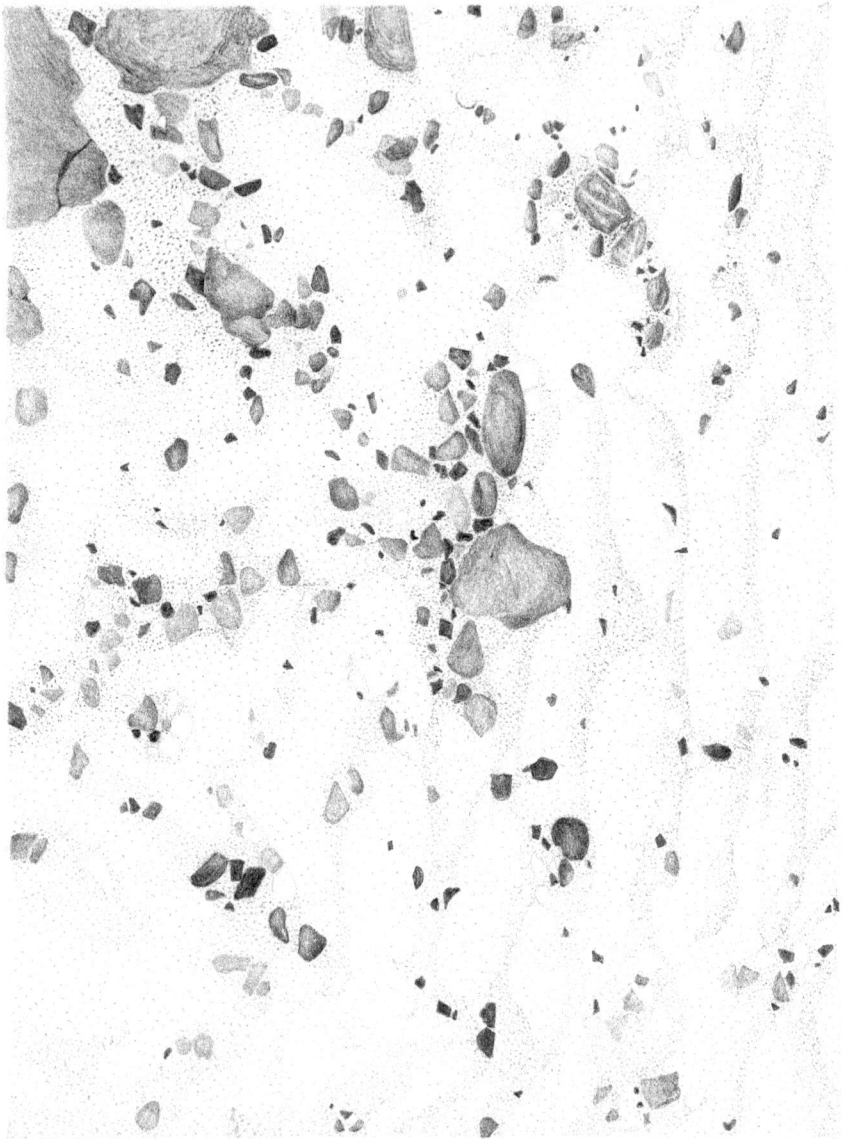

Chapter 9

On Love

A young man had for a certain time been in love with a woman and was convinced that he in her had found the love of his life. On the occasion of her approaching birthday, he had bought a present he knew would please her. He had arranged for dinner in an expensive restaurant. Through the days leading up to her birthday, he had given much thought to how he, during the dinner, could declare his love. Using the three words "I love you" seemed to him to be at once too banal and too intimate. For the duration of the dinner he searched for words, but found only banalities and clichés. At one point, his eye fell on a bowl of marshmallows, and he spontaneously exclaimed: "I marshmallow you". The beloved tenderly replied that she had never received such a poetic declaration of love. The story comes from Alain de Botton's[1] charming book on love.

De Botton's story reminds us that love cannot belong to everyday conceptual language, just as we do not expect it to be treated in scientific essays. Rather, we turn to literature and philosophy when we want to know more about love than our own life experience tells us. The language of love does not only resist scientific discourse. The language of love is, as Julia Kristeva writes, "a flight of metaphors – it is literature".[2] Even in our everyday encounters with love, we prefer figurative to conceptual language when we wish to put our love for another into words, for example creating the metaphor "I marshmallow you", or like Swann in Marcel Proust's *Remembrance of Things Past* says to his beloved Odette: "You don't mind if I straighten the flowers in your bodice",[3] referring to the first time they had driven home together and her flowers in her corsage had been upset. Doing a cattleya remained their preferred metaphor for making love.

Although we today regard declarations of everlasting romantic love as antiquated and a little grandiloquent, out of touch with the way we live and understand love today, the fantasy of life-long love is still alive across generations and is only reinforced by its being so difficult to realise. The inherent contradictions of love have been regarded and explored as an aspect of cultural development, the idea of love twisted and turned in Plato's *Symposium*, and psychoanalysts from Freud to Lacan have contributed with analyses of the origin and development of love. Finally, love has been interpreted in a Christian and ethical perspective, as we shall see.

In his classic work *Love in the Western World*, Denis de Rougemont[4] traces the concept of love of our culture back to the troubadour poets of the 10th century. Besides being an important work on the cultural history of love, the writer builds his work on a thorough acquaintance with the work of Freud. Our conceptions of love, writes de Rougemont, are based on an expectancy of passion, a literary idea introduced by the figure of Tristan, praised by the troubadour poets at the end of the 10th century. It survives in the romantic concept of love that has been so decisive for the understanding of love in western culture that one could, with an aphorism borrowed from la Rochefoucauld, say that some people would never have fallen in love if they had not heard there were such a thing.[5]

Love is passion, and passion means suffering. However, according to de Rougemont, the problem arises when passion, belonging to the sphere of the sacred and sublime, is profaned. What began as the myth of passionate love, created through relinquishment, was in de Rougemont's words democratised and through the same process lost its aesthetic and spiritual value. This has entailed the paradox that we today seek the passion of unrequited and un-attainable love, but only as fiction, never as a fate pursued in our personal love lives. Tristanism lives its subversive life in our yearnings and colours our de-sires, but disturbs the happiness we find so difficult to find in life-long re-lationships. When passion becomes profane and thus loses its sublime and sacral dimension, it can even become destructive, writes de Rougemont. He regards the contemporary break-down of marriage as a sign of this profanation of passion and reads it as an expression of the medieval conflict between the heretical movements and Christian orthodoxy. This contradiction has left us with two forms of morality, for which the crisis of modern marriage is an expression. The first morality secures the preservation of family and society; the second sings the praises of passion, although the song is muted and the expression profaned, not to say perverted.

Freud would obviously have joined in this exploration of the cultural and historical idea of love. However, in accordance with his science, he chose to study the psycho-sexual foundations of the split in love he had ample possi-bility to observe in his patients. His contribution to the understanding of the complicated love lives of humans was not written with a poetic pen. Freud's rationalism and his scientific ambition contributed to his point of entry to the understanding of love, which was not passion, but rather the structure and dynamics of fantasy. There was however one place, where passionate love entered the psychoanalytic stage. In the transference, the analysand not only spoke of his/her longings for love, but brought love into the relationship to the analyst.

In his three brief essays on love,[6] Freud writes on the complications of love life inspired by his clinical experience with patients, adding to this his theoretical corpus, particularly his theory of the Oedipus complex and the incest taboo. He introduces these texts with an admission of the advantage of the poet relative to the scientist, when it comes to describing love. Dealing with love and its prerequisites in the choice of love object has been the poet's privilege, he writes. The poet, however, is bound to the aim of aesthetic pleasure. To this Freud adds that the poet is to a lesser extent interested in the origin and development of love into its final form in the individual subject. After this admission of the poet's privilege in the field of love, Freud in these three essays describes and analyses the split in human love life that we know from our own lives.

Through a masculine lens, and with the background theory of the Oedipus complex and incest taboo, Freud describes how the masculine subject's love reaches the height of passion when the object of his love is unattainable, or impossible due to oedipal rivalry, or when the woman appears sexually questionable. If the woman belongs to another, rivalry can be the force responsible for the intensification of the man's desire, while for others prostitutes stimulate desire and increase drive pressures. The tendency of jealousy to intensify love is masterfully described in Marcel Proust's novel *Remembrance of Things Past,*[7] where the protagonist is driven by jealousy, attempting to guess the hidden desires of his beloved, her Gomorrah character, becoming a detective as well as a researcher. It is the secret desire of his beloved Albertine that binds him to a relationship where he suffers more than he enjoys, and where his tender feelings for her are the result of appeasement rather than love.

Masculine drive satisfaction seems contingent on the tendency towards debasement of the love object, which for some men means that when they desire, they cannot love, and when they love, they cannot desire. An explanation to this "debasement in the sphere of love" is found, regarding the male subject, in the fact that the mother, as first love object, remains an idealised image, which stands in the way of uninhibited sexual satisfaction. It is somewhat different for the woman, who also takes her mother as her first love object, but later displaces her love onto her father, simultaneously identifying with the mother. While the man, throughout his life, retains the woman as his love object, the girl, in her development into womanhood, replaces the love for her mother with love for her father. For the man, the image of his mother often casts a shadow over the women he later falls in love with and binds himself to, while the girl, throughout her development into a woman, struggles with the problem that she is to separate from her mother as well as identify with her, while her relationship to her father is less ambiguous. The woman often brings this whole complex process into her later love relationships, where it is manifested as frustration and demands on the man to live up to a love she in fantasy links to an idealised father. Both sexes, however, share the difficulty of integrating drive satisfaction with the need for love.

The splitting of love life, and its consequences, are explained by psychoanalysis in the light of two basic preconditions. The first consists in love's containing a sensual as well as an affectionate current. These do not always accompany each other, and their respective developments markedly differ. The second precondition is the assumption that there is something in the nature of the drive that resists its satisfaction. The human need for love, writes Freud, entirely in accordance with de Rougemont, apparently requires "[an obstacle] in order to heighten the libido; and where natural resistances to satisfaction have not been sufficient men have at all times erected conventional ones so as to be able to enjoy love".[8] I shall return to the question of this something, that hinders desire from attaining the heights of passion, and as we shall see, is related to the nature of the drive, which is more complex than we would perhaps like to think.

One of the keys to understanding the split between the drive and love lies in the very concept of the sexual drive that Freud gradually developed and that began with his asking himself the question of how we should understand a drive and what makes sexuality a drive. To this purpose, a reckoning with two prejudices on sexuality was necessary. The first was the idea that human sexuality serves procreation, while the second consisted in the wish to see the drive's advent as concurrent with the sexual maturation of puberty. The idea of infantile sexuality revolutionised the understanding of sexuality. By separating drive and instinct, and defining the drive as the interface of the somatic and the psychic, Freud could demonstrate that the small child, throughout its early development, experiences a form of pleasure linked to different and separate parts of the body, from the oral to the anal and phallic. He showed that from the oral instinctual satisfaction of hunger through sucking, the independent pleasure of sucking, while leaning on the instinct, breaks off and becomes independent from hunger, where after the child begins to suck things other than the mother's breast. From sucking out of need, the child begins to suck for pleasure. The same leaning on and differentiation from the instinct is observed in all the other so-called partial drives, which besides the oral and anal encompass the body as a whole, which when stimulated beyond a certain level, produces pleasure. We know this not least from sports activities, and equally, intellectual activity which can be conducive to pleasure.

Freud introduced the concept of polymorphous perverse sexuality to denote this infantile form of pleasure and assumed that this pleasure endures and, under normal circumstances, makes up part of what we understand as mature genital satisfaction. Under particular circumstances, this development, however, does not take place. Polymorphous sexuality is not integrated into genital sexuality, but is fixated on the infantile level and expressed in what we term the perversions.

Love develops along a completely different path and has its source in the early relationships between the child and the people who care for it. This infantile form of love is characterised by being exclusive and is doomed to die. As opposed to the drive, the object of which is interchangeable, love chooses its object, elevating and idealising it, as in the first flush of romantic infatuation, and thus testifies to the developmental basis of romantic love, a concept described by de Rougemont and many others. The love objects we choose as adults will always be replacements for this forever lost and eternally desired object. There is a beautiful description of the transformation from infatuation in Stendahls three-volume work on love.[9] He uses a metaphor, and speaks of crystallisation, when he describes how love comes into existence. In Salzburg a branch, denuded of its leaves by winter, writes Stendahl, is thrown into the desolate depth of a salt mine; two to three months later, it is retrieved and is at this point covered with glimmering crystals. Applied to love, crystallisation takes two forms. At the first crystallisation, the man adores and elevates the woman of whose love he thinks himself assured, while anticipating his happiness with boundless pleasure. The passion is so powerful, and the desire equally so, that it gives itself away in the smallest of signs. In the following crystallization doubts and insecurities about the mutuality of love are what create passion, and sustain it.

I have in the preceding used the concepts of drive and desire without differentiating between them. It is, however, important to discriminate between drive and desire in order to understand what it is that prevents passion from reaching fulfilment. While the drive is directed toward the object, and will always find gratification in the body's partial erogenous zones, if it does not find satisfaction in relation to a love object, desire is directed – not toward another object, but another subject. When desire is focused on another subject, another person, it is not the gratification of the drives that is essential, but the uncertainty and anxiety related to the question of what the desiring subject means to the other. The dilemma of love, in other words, is the importance I have for the one I love. As desiring subjects, we are in a position of vulnerability, since the other holds the answer to the question of my worth. What do I mean? What am I worth to the other?

The dissolution of the concept of the drive into drive and desire, respectively, is French psychoanalyst Jacques Lacan's merit. He thus made it possible to expand the understanding of the split between the sensual and affectionate currents of love, introduced by Freud in his brief psychological essays on love. We have thus acquired a psychoanalytical counterpart of de Rougemonts historical exploration of passionate love. It is desire that makes love passionate, since desire is characterised by its mobility, being displaced from one object to another. We might think that we can satisfy desire by being granted our wishes, but our experience shows us that the gratification of wishes does not bring the expected fulfilment. Desire does not seek gratification, because this would put an end to pleasure. Desire, and its concurrent abstinence from immediate gratification, is the guarantee that our needs can be civilised or cultivated.

The path of development of the drive and of love both leave humans with a longing for the first and lost object of the drives and of love. This double loss is inscribed as a lack in our psyches, and this lack has particular consequences for love life, or more specifically, for what we understand by loving another human being. I will return to this, and here conclude my observations on loss and longing with an ancient fable. In Plato's *Symposium*, a tribute to Eros, the philosopher attributes the following words to Aristophanes, the ancient comedian: "Once, human beings were endowed with double bodies, with four arms and four legs, displacing themselves by doing cartwheels. Their sex could be masculine, or feminine, or both, as every human was endowed with two sets of genitals. These creatures became threatening to the gods, and Zeus therefore decided to divide them in two, thus creating humanity as we know it. Since then, every human being searches for its "missing half", and depending on sex, yearns for a return to an original state by finding either a man or a woman. If we are not careful, we risk being cleft once more, while we conversely hope to return to our primal state if we behave well.[10] We thus seek lost unity, and Eros is an expression for this quest, since sexuality is what brings us closest to our first state. Aristophanes description of the original and lost wholeness is not devoid of humour, just as his speech is generally coloured by a relaxed humour. The image of original man, who can only move by doing cartwheels, is obviously linked to the vicissitudes of sex. Are we one, two or several sexes, and how are we, in consequence, to behave? Does Aristophanes want us to smile at the troubles of sexual life, or on the contrary, is he deeply serious, with the help of a mythical explanatory model?

I choose to interpret him in the latter way, and suggest that he transfers the question of what love is, using a different language than the conceptual one. With his comical tale of human longing, the poet treats the basically tragic predicament that we are, from birth, separated from our first object of love and from then on doomed to seek our missing half, in our culture recreated in the imagery of romantic love. It is the experience of lost unity, which Aristophanes has captured as comedy, a genre that he mastered.

I will dwell on Plato's *Symposium*, as also Socrates, in his speech on love, borrows the voice of another. Referring to a conversation with the wise priestess Diotima, Socrates lets the woman speak of love in his place, and in the evolving exchange with her, loss appears as the central theme of love. This is rendered as the love encounter between the woman Penia and the man Porus. She is a poor girl, who owns nothing, but conceives a child with the drunk Porus. It is obvious that Penia, who has nothing, is the one who gives love. She even gives birth to the child on the same day that Aphrodite comes to the world. Therefore, we hear, love has always had a particular affinity with beauty. I return to the idea of love and beauty after a reference to Lacan, for whom the fable of Penia and Porus was decisive to the discussion of love and for the paradoxical and thought-provoking statement he formulated as an afterthought to Diotima's fable: "Love is giving what you don't have",[11] a statement in direct contradiction to Aristophanes claim in *Symposium*, that "you can't give to another what you don't have yourself",[12] a statement that seems intuitively more adequate.

Lacan's provocative statement should be read in light of lack, previously explained as the result of the loss of the object of the drive as well as the object of love. Lack is, furthermore, a basic assumption in Lacan's understanding of the subject, linked to the introduction into the symbolic order. In other words, it is language that marks the transition from connectedness with the other, or, put another way, language separates the child from the original at-oneness with the first object. At that moment, desire emerges, striving to fill the lack. Our later wishes are attempts to fill this lack and re-find the situation when the child was one with another, as Aristophanes visualised in his speech. The many disappointments we experience throughout our love lives testify to the impossibility of completely satisfying desire. Lack is however also what drives us in the eternal attempt to be someone particular, to be the one and only for another human being. The concept of lack should not only be understood as negative. It belongs to every subject as something unique and precious, not to be given away lightly. When we open ourselves in love for another, when we love someone, it is out of this lack, and the yearning and longing tied to it with the expectation that the other will receive it. When we say to another that we love him or her, it means, following this line of thought, that we open ourselves to the other with the lack we carry, trusting that the other will recognise and care for this vulnerability, and conversely, when we fall in love with and love the other, it is because we intuit that the other, out of his lack, will give back what we have given the beloved.

In contrast to desire, loving entails the expectation of being loved in return. "To love is, essentially, to wish to be loved" writes Lacan.[13] This does not mean that we demand of the other that he or she love us back, but rather that we, in opening ourselves in the recognition of our lack endow the other with a gift, not in the sense of a material gift, or symbolic token of our devotion. It is our deepest and most vulnerable being we cloak in the words with which we declare our love. We thus expect the other to accept and treasure this gift, and love us in return. When we express our love, speaking words of love, it means that the other has touched my innermost being, and become an intimate part of myself. That which is called the miracle of love, and to most of us appears inexplicable and enigmatic, can in light of these observations be understood as the reaching out of one human toward another, and this other spontaneously reciprocating this gesture, thus creating the spark that strikes us with love. When this wonder occurs, it is not so much because these two people are captivated by each other as because they are both situated at the very heart of the miracle of love. Of this spark, Proust has written, "Among all the methods by which love is brought into being, among all agents which disseminate that blessed bane, there are so few efficacious as this gust of feverish agitation that sweeps over us from time to time. For then the die is cast, the person whose company we enjoy at the moment is the person we shall henceforth love".[14]

I return to Plato, and Diotima's speech which, besides treating lack, links the essence of love to man's ability to perceive and develop the sense of beauty. Here, love is said to belong to the kind of phenomena which do not allow themselves to be unambiguously determined, but is to be found between the knowable and the unknowable, between the ugly and the beautiful. This indeterminacy explains the mysterious character of love. In love, the subject experiences something for which it lacks words, but knows, without necessarily understanding it. From this point, Diotima proceeds into the domain of idealised, or sublimated, love. The reader understands that Plato is speaking through Socrates and the wise woman. In this form, love has nothing to do with ownership, but belongs to being and to the creativity of being. The real purpose of love is "giving birth in beauty, whether in body or soul",[15] says the priestess. Even if such a process contains an element of pain, whether through childbirth or a spiritual birth, it is also what can carry a subject beyond fragility and finitude, giving rise to the illusion of immortality. By seeking beauty as part of being, man undergoes a transformation in the very kernel of his self, which makes him lovable not only to others, but also to himself. I might venture to say that man's quest for beauty adds an aspect to love that might be called sublime.

Many objections could be raised to Lacan's statement that *loving is giving what one does not have*. But because I find it valuable and important to reflect upon, I wish to complement it with a thinker who has a similar reflection. I turn to Søren Kierkegaard and his thoughts in *Works of Love*,[16] whereupon I will attempt to show what such a conception of love can mean for the work of psychoanalysis, the aim of which was once described as making man capable of love and work.

In Kierkegaard, the concept of love is extended from the one and only to fellow man. An exploration of love of fellow man will add some essential aspects to the idea of love, not least since it inscribes love into an ethical discourse. Temporarily setting the predominantly psychoanalytic discussion of love aside, let us focus on Kierkegaard's Christian view of the love of one's neighbour, beginning with Freud's acutely critical view on love of fellow man. In *Civilization and its Discontents* (1930), Freud discusses the biblical commandment that urges us to love our neighbour as ourselves. Firstly, he argues, this is a mockery of love. The universalism here expressed runs counter to the nature of love. Not everybody is deserving of our love. In Freud's own words: "A love that does not discriminate seems to me to forfeit a part of its own value, by doing injustice to its object; and secondly, not all men are worthy of love".[17] Secondly, he regards the commandment of love for the other, which he calls the most recent command of the cultural superego, as the source of unhappiness, being an unrealistic command that makes people fall ill in neurosis. The demand to love fellow man to this extent overlooks the fact that a quantum of drive satisfaction is implicit to love, and that there are limits to the extent of drive renunciation of which humans are capable. Thirdly and most importantly, the view of man on which the command to love one's neighbour rests is hollow. The dictate functions as an illusion concealing the fact that humans are not only love-seeking creatures and that their drives contain a good portion of aggression. Nonetheless, Freud admits that love of fellow man constitutes a form of love separate from sexual love in the sense that love of fellow man disregards whether the other has made himself deserving of my love. Lacan follows Freud when he insists that it is precisely the tendencies to torment and kill the other that underlay the command. The commandment to love one's neighbour as oneself forces man to confront destructive aspects in himself and in others, aspects that we are keen to repress, deny and find excuses for.

Let us look at how Kierkegaard treats the commandment to love one's neighbour as oneself. I will limit myself to two aspects of Kierkegaard's detailed exploration of the commandment. First, I examine what exactly is meant by neighbour, and secondly, what it means to love one's neighbour *as oneself*. The commandment to love one's neighbour as oneself implies that I love myself. This is not to be understood as conceit or as narcissism. How I love myself is not indifferent. But would it not be possible to love another higher than oneself, asks Kierkegaard. This is the stuff of which poets write. But the love that the poets praise, claims the Danish philosopher, is essentially the same as self-love, finding its intoxicating expression in the words of the poet. The ingenious expression *as thyself* comes dangerously close to self-love, and self-love can only defend itself by creating doubt as to the identity of the neighbour or other. The neighbour is physically nearest to the self and is thus the one or several others closest to us. But not in the sense that they are the preferential ones. Choosing the other on the grounds of preference, writes Kierkegaard, is nothing but an expression of self-love, which has elevated itself to the position of judge, a statement worth remembering in a time when choosing on the grounds of preference has become a marked trait in political and public discourse, separating them from us; the foreign which does not belong to us from those we in our self-aggrandisement call our neighbours. The neighbour is practically a double of the self. The neighbour can be understood, writes Kierkegaard, as what "the thinkers call 'the other'".[18]

Utilising the lens of psychoanalysis, I would like to claim that loving the other as oneself implies that not only do I love him as foreign, but I also love him in the way I love, and have understood and acknowledged what is foreign in myself. In other words, when we recognise the foreign within ourselves, meaning the destructive and hateful impulses that we would like to repress, we can love our neighbour in the right way. "When the law as yourself has wrested from you the self-love that Christianity sadly enough must presuppose to be in every human being, then you have actually learned to love yourself. The Law is therefore: You shall love yourself in the same way as you love your neighbor when you love him as yourself".[19]

When Freud is critical towards the commandment of love for fellow man, it is because of the concept's lack of boundaries. It is the only Christian commandment formulated as such, with the explicit formulation *thou shalt*, and not as a prohibition, which means that it lacks boundaries. However, these two words are also used in other ways, such as when we scold our children that they must remember to brush their teeth or take off their shoes. The expression *thou shalt* thus comes to signify something in the direction of what you should do because you can and because it represents a humane gesture which is possible as well as appropriate.

Freud's criticism can also be explained in light of the dyadic, imaginary model of love that he assumes. In love we mirror ourselves in the other, and love is primarily treated as a relation between two individuals. When Kierkegaard speaks of what the other is "other" in relation to, what is implied is not the other individual, but the relation to the third, which for Kierkegaard is God. That is to say that in our otherness towards God, all humans are alike. In other words, the relation to God as a third term, makes us equal. We recognise the Platonic ideal of love as a third term between good and evil, between the ugly and the beautiful. In other words, something stands between the subject and the other, and one is tempted to ask what happens to love of fellow man when the relation to God crumbles. One immediate thought is that this might result in the individual regarding himself as divine, with the self, in its aggrandisement, taking on the functions of God as creator of law and arbitror, with all the guilt and self-reproaches that this entails. With the raising of man to divinity there is no longer an external agent that can ease our suffering, and in which we can seek solace and forgiveness. This is the ethic that is implicit in Kierkegaard's *Works of Love*. I would also like to claim that it is the ethic underlying the setting of the psychoanalytic cure.

In his writings on love, Freud attempted to explain the emergence and development of love, and in clinical work, he directly experienced the outbreak of love at the heart of analytic work. When a female patient suddenly flung her arms around him and kissed him, Freud was sober enough to realise that this sudden and passionate gesture could not be ascribed to his personal charms, but on the contrary must be something created by the cure. No doubt, it contained a measure of love, but love as an *artefact*, and as such, engendered by the cure, conceptualised as transference love. It is the analyst, Freud concludes, who has conjured this love into being, by offering the analytical setting, with the objective of curing neurosis. What boldness! Psychoanalysis was, in other words, created as a cure of love.

Transference love does not necessarily present itself in the direct and passionate form with which the hysterical patients responded to treatment, but is in its more subtle and quiet forms a constant and significant part of the cure. But what does it really mean, that love manifests itself as transference? What is transference, and how is the demand for love answered in analysis? Transference is often depicted as a one-way communication from the analysand to the analyst, and as that around which everything revolves. As a consequence, the transference has become the locus of the most important aspect of analytical work. Here, however, there is a risk of placing the person of the analyst in a central position and of overlooking the fact that the transference is not directed to the analyst personally, but to what the analysand sees in the analyst – not what is evident, but on the contrary, what is hidden. Paraphrasing Picasso's statement that he in his art does not seek, but finds, one could say the same of the analysand. She finds the space within the analyst that mirrors and manifests her lack. This presupposes that the analyst meets the analysand with an openness to his or her own lack.

Transference has also been understood as the repetition of the patterns of love we carry within us since childhood. This is, however, a simplification. Transference is never a repetition of the same. In the transference, the analysand creates what French psychoanalyst Jean Laplanche has termed a *hollow*[20] – a space where the original, past situation can be recreated. Hollowness must also characterise the analyst, who opens herself to her analysand without knowledge or desire. The analyst thus meets the patient with an attitude that could be called benevolent neutrality. As an analyst, I come to care for my analysands. I have empathy, sympathy and great respect for the work they do in analysis. But while it is the privilege of the analysand to love her analyst with one of the many forms of love, it is the analyst's task to abstain from being loving, as well as from being the one supposed to know. One expression of this is in the analyst's silence. Not in the sense that the analyst says nothing, but because the analyst is aware that that every utterance brings the analysand's attention to the analyst, and to what he/she might desire from her analysand, the analyst remains silent until she can formulate a reply to that which the analysand seeks.

The task of the analyst in other words consists of making herself available as the one who, according to the analysand, is "supposed to know", as Lacan has expressed it. This does not make the analyst the one who knows better. Just as the analysand is incapable of speaking of that which is hidden in the unconscious, and therefore needs another to express it, the analyst must also speak from a position of not knowing. The creation of such a subtle and indirect dialogue requires ethical imperatives. Lacan[21] has formulated this by claiming that the status of the unconscious is ethical. This should not be understood as the unconscious being ethical, but rather that questions emanating from the speech of the unconscious require not only a reply, but also imply the responsibility of caring for, of nurturing and answering the questions of the unconscious with tact and sensitivity.

Notes

1 De Botton, A. (2006). *Essays in Love*. New York: Grove Press/Atlantic Monthly Press.
2 Kristeva, J. (1983). *Tales of Love*. New York: Columbia University Press.

3 Proust, M., & Proust, M. (1871–1922/1982). *Remembrance of Things Past,* Vol. 1, p. 254. New York: Random House, Vintage Books.

4 De Rougemont, D. (1940/1983). *Love in the Western World.* Princeton, New Jersey: Princeton University Press.

5 De la Rochefoucauld, F. (1817/2008). *Collected Maxims and Other Reflections.* Oxford, England: Oxford University Press.

6 Freud, S. A Special Type of Object Choice Made by Men (1910), On the Universal Tendency to Debasement in the Sphere of Love (1912), and The Taboo of Virginity (1918). *The Standard Edition of the Complete Psychological Works,* Vol. XI. London: The Hogarth Press.

7 Proust, M. (1871–1922/1981). *Remembrance of Things Past,* Vol. I. New York: Random House, Vintage Books.

8 Freud, S. (1912). On the Universal Tendency to Debasement in the Sphere of Love. *The Standard Edition of the Complete Psychological Works,* Vol. XI, p. 187. London: The Hogarth Press.

9 Stendahl. (1822/1975). *On Love.* London, Penguin Classics.

10 Plato. (1989). *Symposium.* Translated by A. Nehamas & P. Woodruff. Indianapolis & Cambridge: Hackett Publishing Company.

11 Fink, B. (2016). *Lacan on Love. An Exploration of Lacan's Seminar VIII, Transference.* Cambridge: Polity Press.

12 Plato. (1989). *Symposium,* p. 35. Translated by A. Nehamas & P. Woodruff. Indianapolis & Cambridge: Hackett Publishing Company.

13 Lacan, J. (1978). *Seminar XI. The Four Fundamental Concepts of Psychoanalysis,* p. 253. New York, London: W.W. Norton & Company.

14 Proust, M. *Remembrance of Things Past,* Vol. I, p. 252. New York: Random House, Vintage Books.

15 Plato. (1989). *Symposium,* p. 53. Translated by A. Nehamas & P. Woodruff. Indianapolis & Cambridge: Hackett Publishing Company.

16 Kierkegaard, S. (1998). *Works of Love.* Edited and translated by H.V. Hong & E.H. Hong. Princeton, New Jersey: Princeton University Press.

17 Freud, S. (1930). Civilization and its Discontents. *The Standard Edition of the Complete Psychological Works of Sigmund Freud,* Vol. XXI, p. 102. London: The Hogarth Press.

18 Kierkegaard, S. (1998). *Works of Love,* p. 21. Edited and translated by H.V. Hong & E.H. Hong. Princeton, New Jersey: Princeton University Press.

19 Kierkegaard, S. (1998). *Works of Love,* pp. 22–23. Edited and translated by H.V. Hong & E.H. Hong. Princeton, New Jersey: Princeton University Press.

20 Laplanche, J. (1999). Transference: Its Provocation by the Analyst. In: *Essays on Otherness.* London: Routledge.

21 Lacan, J. (1978). *Seminar XI. The Four Fundamental Concepts of Psychoanalysis.* New York, London: W.W. Norton & Company.

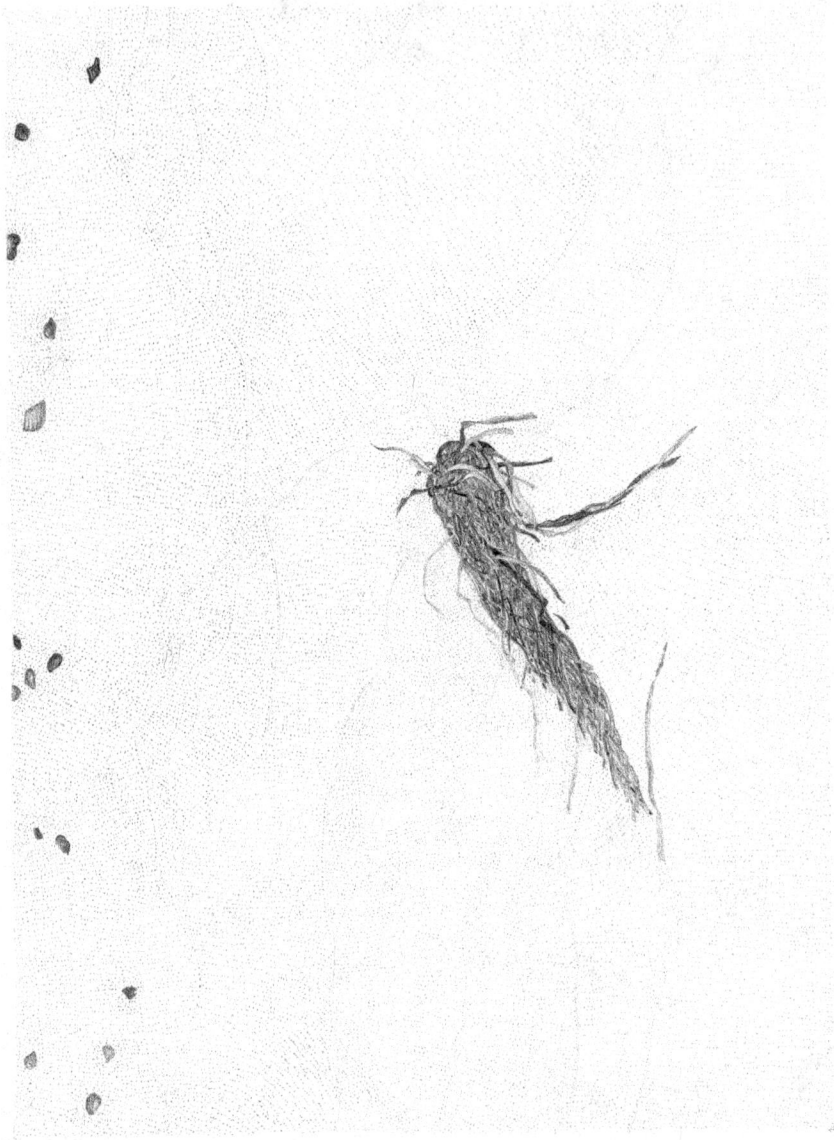

Chapter 10

The uncanny

It is not unusual that sudden changes occur during analytic work, where what previously seemed known and familiar is replaced by the unknown and alien. During the first encounters with a patient, an outline generally appears of something which resembles a life history, punctuated by significant events and the names of important people in the patient's life. This is followed by a shift; the story is blurred, and our immediate understanding loses its power of conviction. The previously so clearly defined personality becomes foreign, and the landscape in which analyst and analysand dwell becomes clouded and unclear. Later, the landscape usually becomes less vague; patterns are discernible, and new shapes appear in the interminable work on thoughts, language and dreams. The foreign and unknown landscape points to the processes at work in the unconscious, which follow completely different laws from those governing consciousness. The unconscious is ruled by the pleasure principle; energy flows freely with the help of the mechanisms of condensation and displacement, through which the deepest wishes of the mind can find a path to a fulfilment of sorts.

There is, however, another kind of strangeness, with which it is more difficult to familiarise oneself and which touches on the uncanny. With time, Freud was increasingly attentive to this aspect of the unconscious, and in 1920, with his text *Beyond the Pleasure Principle,*[1] he took the consequences of these insights into the darker corners of psychic life, revised his drive theory, and introduced the concept of the death drive. More interesting than the speculative idea of a death drive is the clinical experience of repetition, for which the death drive was a theoretical answer. The repetition here referred to is different from the one manifested in the transference and in the work with the patient's free associations or dreams. While the latter could be called a repetition of the same, the kind of repetition that was conceptualised as the repetition compulsion is something entirely different. What is in question here is the repetition of the identical, a repetition with no other aim than repetition itself. This form of repetition is clearly manifested in psychological symptoms, which, seen from the perspective of the ego, appear alien. The symptoms live their own compulsive lives, without any consideration for reason or reality.

Something repeats itself in the symptom with such a blind and obsessive force that Freud, in his essay of 1920, spoke of a demonic aspect, which seemed to adhere not only to the symptoms of his patients, but to the entire way of life of certain people.

The year preceding the formulation of the repetition compulsion, Freud had, in his exploration of the phenomenon of the uncanny,[2] the possibility to acquaint himself with the phenomenon of repetition. Freud's essay demonstrates that he is in search of something, which would, however, not be completed until the following year with the text *Beyond the Pleasure Principle*. The text on the uncanny is a fine example of how Freud attempts to come to grasps with a phenomenon which would not, unresistingly, be incorporated into the psychoanalytical conceptual frame – as if the phenomenon itself resisted every attempt at understanding. It insisted, in a way, on remaining alien. In his exploration of the uncanny, Freud found himself confronted with something more alien than the pathological variations of the human mind that his clinical experience had familiarised him with.

The theory of the death drive and the concept of repetition compulsion are not only present in *The "Uncanny"*, but probably play a not unimportant part in the very elaboration of the material Freud worked with, and not least, repetition is manifested in the difficulty Freud's text displays in coming to a conclusion. It is as if he were waiting for an insight, that could be formulated first in *Beyond the Pleasure Principle*. Since he, in his exploration of the uncanny, bound himself to a particular interpretation of the story, which is presented as the model of the uncanny, he shut something out of his explanation, something which appears in several places in the text – not as actual answers, but as new questions. There was something indefinite haunting Freud in his exploration of the uncanny, which compelled him, like Scheherazade, to make repeated additions to his story.

Freud's text thus shows that form is not just external with respect to content, but is inherent to the creation of the addressed theme. He experienced this already when he, in collaboration with Josef Breuer in the 1890s worked on *Studies in Hysteria*, where it was shown that the recorded case studies more resembled novels than medical records. There was something inherent in the object of exploration, writes Freud time and again, that intruded into the very nature of the examination and stylistically coloured it. In a letter to his friend Fliess, Freud wrote about his *Interpretation of Dreams* that although he could vouch for everything he presented in this major work, there was something in the very style that repelled him. It was, doubtless, this recognition of how the very subject of examination wrote itself into his text, that made Freud the great essayist he was, which is so convincingly demonstrated in The Uncanny. The literary form of the essay offered itself as the medium that brought Freud's psychoanalytic thinking to life. *The "Uncanny"* is not only the formulation of a factual relationship, but also the expression of the subject writing itself through the very form of the rendition.

There are other reasons to acquaint oneself with Freud's text on *The "Uncanny"*. The phenomenon reveals itself to be much more inclusive than Freud at first assumed, and the many examples, pulled together as evidence, are not immediately coherent. Freud was therefore compelled to constantly adopt new points of view, to put new assumptions to the test, in his attempt to clarify the contradictions he encountered. The result is that we, as readers, are invited into a space of experimental thinking and can therefore witness Freud's dialogue with himself in the attempt to grasp his material and a phenomenon which appears enigmatic throughout the entire text.

The "Uncanny" is moreover interesting, as it displays Freud as the reader of literary text, in this case the romantic author E.T.A. Hoffmann's story of *The Sandman*,[3] which was read as an allegory of the uncanny. Freud's literary interest was vast and legendary. He had earlier made use of mythological material, not least of Sophocles' rendition of the Oedipus myth, which was to become the linchpin of his theory of development of the personality. He was deeply fascinated with Shakespeare, Dostoevsky, Goethe and Ibsen, from whom he was inspired, and whom he envied for their intuitive grasp of the very material that he had far greater trouble in giving shape to. *The "Uncanny"* is exemplary as a classical psychoanalytical reading of a piece of literature. This reading has not stood unquestioned. Freud's essay was read and criticised by psychoanalysts as well as literary scholars, and their criticism can be said to confirm the unfinished character of Freud's treatment of the phenomenon of "the uncanny". This criticism does not necessarily weaken Freud's analysis, but opens for other angles regarding the nature of the uncanny.

The exploration of the uncanny falls into three parts. First, a lexical and etymological examination of the words "Heimlich" and "Unheimlich" is undertaken, which rapidly is shown to lead to the important hypothesis that "… this uncanny is in reality nothing new or alien, but something which is familiar and old-established in the mind […]".[4] Freud's point of departure thus was that "Heimlich" and "Unheimlich" were not opposites, but that Heimlich, in itself, contains a semantic ambivalence, as the word connotes the familiar as well as the concealed. In this context, Freud cites Schelling, who defines the uncanny as that which should have remained secret but which has come to light.

In the second part of the text, Freud has abandoned the previous philological discussion, and chosen an empirically descriptive approach to instances – be they persons, things, impressions or situations – which with particular acuity illustrate the uncanny. Freud begins with a thesis, articulated by his colleague Jentsch, who had proposed that the uncanny springs from an insecurity about our judgement, when faced with phenomena that we cannot convincingly place as either fantasised or real, such as the insecurity whether a creature is alive or dead. Freud found evidence for his criticism of this thesis in his interpretation of *The Sandman*, which in Freud's eyes came to constitute the model of the uncanny, as it is not the lifeless doll, Olympia, in Hoffmann's short story, that incorporates the uncanny, but the Sandman, an adventurous figure who is said to throw sand in the eyes of naughty children.

Freud opens his narration of *The Sandman* with the story of the student Nathaniel's childhood memories. Despite the joy of his engagement to Clara, Nathaniel is unable to free himself from the memories of his father's horrifying death. Some nights, his mother would urge the children to bed early with the admonishment: "*The Sandman is coming*", and the boy, every time, heard the heavy steps of a visitor who on these evenings claimed the father's exclusive attention. When asked about the Sandman, the mother firmly denied his existence other than as a figure of speech, but the nurse knew better: "He's a wicked man who comes when children won't go to bed, and throws handfuls of sand into their eyes so that they jump out of their heads all bleeding".[5] Driven by the desire to see with his own eyes, the boy managed to spy on the father and his strange guest and saw that the Sandman was none other than Coppelius, the lawyer, a prominent figure from which the children recoiled, when he occasionally came for dinner. The little spy heard Coppelius call: "Eyes, bring eyes! (Hoffmann, 1982 p. 91)". The boy's scream gave him away, and Coppelius, seizing him, threatened to throw smouldering embers from the fire into his eyes. A deep helplessness and long period of illness concludes this episode. The story's narration leaves it unclear whether we are dealing with the anxious boy's frenzied imagination, or with an account, which in the subjective world of imagination has a kind of reality. During a later visit from the Sandman, the father was killed by an explosion in his study.

Nathaniel now claims to recognise the dreaded figure of his childhood in an itinerant optician by the name of Coppola, who has, with Nathaniel's teacher, professor Spalanzani, constructed a mechanical doll, Olympia, with whom Nathaniel falls so violently in love that he shuns his fiancée, the wise and level-headed Clara. Nathaniel appears in Spalanzani´s home at a point where the two inventors are fighting over the doll. The optician has just carried the eyeless doll away, and Spalanzani gathers Olympia's "bloody eyes", throwing them at Nathaniel and claiming that Coppola has stolen them from him. Nathaniel is once again seized by madness, in which memories of his father's death link with newer impressions. After a long convalescence, Nathaniel decides to marry his fiancée, Clara. On a visit to the high tower of the town hall, Clara sights a figure in the crowded street, which Nathaniel recognises as Coppelius/The Sandman. He is anew struck by frenzy and tries to push Clara from the tower. She is saved by her brother, who rushes to the rescue, while Nathaniel throws himself from the tower.

After this powerfully shortened narration of the plot of Hoffmann's story, Freud does not doubt that the uncanny is linked to the figure of the Sandman and to the image of the eyes being torn out. He must therefore refute the assumption of failing judgement as the explanation for the phenomenon of the uncanny. In his reading of Hoffmann´s story, Freud introduces a technique he has used in his other literary texts and locates a subtext in the story – in

accordance with the method he developed in his *Interpretation of Dreams*. There
is thus a hidden text behind the manifest one, and Freud undertakes an ex-
cavation according to the archaeological model. It is the Sandman who, as a
frightening memory or fantasy, is the key to understanding. Guided by his
clinical experiences, Freud introduces the assumption that in dreams and
fantasies reigns a convertible relation between the eye and the male genital,
and that castration anxiety is a decisive factor in the human psyche. The
conclusion is that Nathaniel's anxiety of losing his eyes is a displaced expression of castration anxiety and, as such, is the explanatory theme of
Hoffmann's short story. In Nathaniel's unconscious, the Sandman replaces the
small child's fantasised image of the feared, castrating father, which is thus split
from the image of the good, beloved father. The Sandman appears as the
uncanny Coppelius, who visited the father in the evenings and had a part in his
death, as the story tells. This uncanny figure is repeated in the couple
Coppola/Spalanzani. Freud sees Nathaniel's obsession with the mechanical
doll as the expression of the boy's feminine attitude toward the father of his
childhood. In his love for the automaton, the young man finds a reflection of
this feminine attitude, and he loves Olympia as the image of his own feminine
identity. As a narcissistic mirror image, Olympia is nothing but Nathaniel's
love for his feminine self. The matter here seems closed, but as previously said,
Freud's essay does not end here. As if he doesn't fully believe in the con-
clusiveness of his explanation, he reaches for new themes, of which all have
the character of repetition or in other ways touch on the uncanny. The examples are, however, only interesting in that they all end in an impasse and
therefore do not contribute to solving the riddle of the uncanny. What is it
Freud is looking for, for which he does not seem to find the key? The explanation of castration anxiety as the underlying pattern of the uncanny, which
the story of the Sandman was intended to prove, obviously was not sufficient.
The numerous examples, added to the phenomenon of the uncanny, create
more confusion than clarity and leave the reader with the impression that this
accumulation of examples has the irrevocable character of repetition. What
remains is doubt about the relevance of the many examples and the fundamental thesis of the uncanny as the return of the repressed. We can approach
the riddle of the unfinished aspect of Freud's text by pointing to its limitations,
seen from a literary and psychoanalytical perspective.

Literary critics have brought attention to the way Freud omitted the narrative strategies and technical specificities that Hoffmann made use of. There is
thus a narrator, that Freud does not mention, who speaks of his ambitions and
desires. This desire includes the writer, the reader and the plot itself.
Hoffmann's text opens in a way that gives the reader the impression that what
is at hand is an epistolary short story. Without introduction or commentary,
we are presented with three letters from Nathaniel to Lothar, Clara's brother.
Here, Nathaniel reveals his childhood memories of Coppelius, or the
Sandman. Two shorter letters follow, in which the narrator suddenly

intervenes and insistently asks the reader, if he/she can imagine the hardships suffered by the protagonist. The reader is soon cognisant that these hardships do not apply so much to Nathaniel as to the author's troubles in beginning his story. The narrator, and beyond him, the author, is confronted with the classical problem of every writer: How to begin the story?

With this introduction, which Freud completely omits, we find an example of the way narrative technique and thematic content are interwoven, and that what is uncanny in the Sandman is a function of the textual surface as well of the depths concealed within. When Freud narrates Hoffmann's short story by going directly to Nathaniel's childhood experiences, he creates an illusion in the reader that Nathaniel's actions and the story's events are much more transparent than Hoffmann's text concedes.

Hoffmann's text is anything but transparent. It is voluminous, clever, extravagant and full of life, passion and emotion. Not least, it impresses with its pictorial character. Technically, Hoffmann's narrative utilises two aesthetic tools. He uses the analogy between poetry and painting and the transformation from sense impression to artistic expression, and he renders his text in a lively, sensory but also dramatic language, with words that colour the contours of the story. The three letters frame the story which, because of numerous rhetorical displacements, repetitions and reversals in combination with violent, colour-saturated scenarios and a row of bizarre words, becomes overwhelming and confusing.

Thematically, the eye metaphor plays an altogether central part in Hoffmann's story, on the imaginary as well as on the symbolic level. But while Freud brought the manifest term eye/loss of eye back to the infantile anxiety of penis/loss of penis, the eye metaphor occupies a much subtler level in Hoffmann's text. And it is not the eye as such, but the severed eye, that is in question. The uncanny is linked to the eye isolated from its bodily belonging.[6] In other words, what is in question here is not the eyes as metaphors for the genitals, nor is it castration, but rather the numerous images of eyes isolated from the body, that persecute the protagonist. The severed eyes are located somewhere between the interacting characters, and they seem to constitute the key to understanding the uncanny effect of the story. Coppola, the optician, speaks of "fine eyes" and shows Nathaniel the many different spectacles he hopes to sell him. Nathaniel cannot wrench himself from the dazzling sight of light refracted in the glass of the spectacles: "[F]laming glances leaped more and more wildly together and directed their blood-red beams into Nathaniel's breast".[7] Because of this, he is gripped by anxiety for what he experiences as a repetition of the smouldering embers which Coppola threatened to throw into the boy's eyes. Finally, Nathaniel buys a spy-glass from Coppola, and with this instrumental extension of the eye, he is able to see Olympia in Spalanzani's flat above. He had visited the professor and his daughter, Olympia – a girl with an "angelic face", but with eyes which seemed to stare, as if lacking vision. At the first sight of these eyes Nathaniel is overwhelmed with an "uncanny" feeling. With the help of Coppola's spy-glass, he becomes a voyeur, and his love for Olympia knows no limits. "The eyes alone seemed to him strangely fixed and dead, yet as the image in the glass grew sharper and sharper it seemed as though beams of moonlight began to rise within them" (ibid. p. 110). Freud is aware of the narcissistic mirror metaphor which is here in question, but he places it within an Oedipal structure, describing it as the inverted Oedipus complex instead of giving it a separate space. Nathaniel's relationship to Olympia is not only a matter of the mirroring of narcissistic love, but also of creating life, of the replication of a flesh-and-blood woman, and of a figure created out of a fevered imagination. The evolving theme throws light on the childhood trauma, and on the question of what occupied the father and Coppelius. What the boy spied was nothing if not the "primal scene" sublimated into the desire to create life out of pure matter. It was bound to end badly, as the two men violated the boundaries of what humans are able to accomplish.

Obsessed with the desire to know what is hidden in the flat above, Nathaniel repeats the primal scene of his childhood. His passionate love transforms the lifeless doll Olympia, and he recreates her as a living woman. And not only does she, like a mirror, reflect his own desire, but she also converts his desire into a deeper insight in himself. "It was only for *me* that her look of love arose and flooded through mind and senses; only in Olympia's love do I find myself again" (ibid. p.117). Not until Nathaniel is confronted with her bloody eyes and empty sockets, does he understand that she is not a living creature but a cold and lifeless doll. The narcissistic, imaginary projection and mirroring repeats itself in relation to the living woman in the character of the beloved Clara, whose cold heart Nathaniel wishes to move and fill with love and warmth. But the attempt to win Clara's heart through desire transformed into poetry proves fatal. In a maternally caring and loving way, she rejects his poems, since she realises that they are not meant for her, but are the expression of a frenzied and unsound imagination. Clara attempts to free her betrothed from what she perceives as the delusions of a sick mind, and through her love repeatedly attempts to return him to the real world. But Nathaniel is obsessed with the idea of a world beyond reason and reality, and convinced that this world is also the world of poetry.

The spy-glass which Nathaniel ends up buying from the optician is an instrument that shortens the distance to the object of desire also becomes an instrument in which the eye is doubled and is thus to seal his fate. When in the tower with Clara, whose eye is caught by a strange figure in the crowd, Nathaniel points the spy-glass towards her and not as Freud mistakenly writes, towards the figure in the street. It is not Coppelius that Nathaniel sees, but Clara, transformed into a lifeless doll with the pale face of death. While Coppola's spy-glass offered an imaginary proximity to the object of desire, the instrument also proves fatal, when desire exceeds the limits of the possible and strives towards secrets beyond it. The desire that drove the father to his death is repeated in the son.

Hoffmann simultaneously exhibits and dramatises the problematic of desire. He reveals how the persistent and insatiable striving to capture the object, which is mistakenly pursued as the source of ultimate satisfaction, is exposed as an illusion, which has its full justification and real meaning in the world of art. The artist can materialise and contextualise his desire, he can choose any setting he wishes. Freud's statement that the uncanny has a particular and privileged mode of expression in the arts is therefore justified. The artist can play with illusions, using the space beyond those boundaries that make the world secure and reliable. Scholars of romantic literature have made the observation that the threatening void beyond our habitual categories is revealed in poetry, through ambiguities, polysemy or irreconcilable contradictions, all of which have a destabilising effect on the reader. Something is in movement, seemingly unable to find its place. The severed eyes in Hoffmann's short story have such a destabilising effect. They are not located in their usual place, they are not fixed, and therefore point to an intermediary space – between fantasy and reality, between life and death and between mystery and rationality.

The importance of emphasising the textual and thematic aspect of Hoffmann's romantic story, and the central role of the eye metaphor, does not depend on rejection of Freud's interpretation, which is decidedly legitimate, but is intended to offer an additional reading strategy, which can elaborate the essence of the uncanny. When Freud omits the literary aspects of the story, he makes an altogether legitimate choice, but overlooks the ambiguity and uncertainty which characterise the uncanny in Hoffmann's story.

Freud's theory of the pivotal role of castration in psychosexual development has its own, inherent limitation, which is illustrated in his interpretation of Nathaniel's fate. When Freud insists on equating the eye and the male genital, he overlooks, firstly, that it is not just the eye which is in question, but the eye severed from its socket. He also overlooks that the eye is the powerful and privileged organ of desire; he ignores the relation between perception and desire and misinterprets the question of what it is the child sees when confronted with the mother's lack. "Anatomy is destiny", writes Freud, but anatomy must neither be reduced to biology nor to physiology, which Freud was inclined to do with the reference to what he called "the biological bedrock", the ultimate basis of sexual difference. The perceived difference between the sexes is structured in accordance with the law of the excluded third – a logic which constitutes a binary relation between presence/absence, reality/fantasy, man/woman. It is a logic that the poet suspends and replaces with the third, the intermediary, which has no place in the logic of either-or, but is located between life and death, between fantasy and reality, like the severed eyes in Hoffmann's story.

While Freud attempted to explain the uncanny with reference to the return of the repressed, contemporary psychoanalysts are occupied with that which cannot return, as it has never found a space, neither in the imaginary nor in the symbolic. This anxiety is thus located on a deeper level, reflecting that which cannot be represented and thus cannot be forgotten or located in the past. Something has happened and has no place to reside, as the British psychoanalyst Donald Winnicott has written, concerning the phenomenon "fear of breakdown".[8] The fear is projected out into reality and into the future, but refers to something past. The French psychoanalyst Jacques Lacan has expressed the same idea, saying that what cannot be represented in the symbolic, appears in the real.

Adding the experience of clinical work with trauma, sexual violations and various other psychological conditions characterised by lack of representation to the discussion of the uncanny, we catch sight of another dimension of the phenomenon. When traumatic experiences, because of their overwhelming character, find no space in the psyche, they can neither be forgotten nor repressed. The only defence for such an experience is a psychic annihilation, rejection or, in psychoanalytic terms, disavowal of the traumatic experience. Such a defence leaves a hole or void in the psyche, provoking anxiety which is qualitatively different from the repetition of the incomprehensible experiences of childhood of which Freud writes, and which I have called repetitions of the same, a repetition with variations, one could say, as opposed to repetition without variation, that is, repetition of the identical. The anxiety that follows from this is not anxiety of anything definite. It is an anxiety which, with a striking expression, could be called nameless dread. The anxiety has no name or existence in language. It is an anxiety of annihilation or emptiness, and in the face of such anxiety, the subject has only the possibility of acting the dreaded nothingness out in destructive or self-destructive actions – as if the only way of warding off the fear is by repeating it, in an identical fashion, in dreams or in acts. We see examples of this today, when soldiers with post-traumatic symptoms find no peace, as the fear-provoking events have found no space in the psyche and therefore cannot be elaborated. They are identically repeated, in a realistic way that is unbearable.

Seen in this light, the uncanny is not, as Freud formulated it in his play on "Heimlich" and "Unheimlich", the secret which should have remained hidden but is now revealed, but, to remain within the metaphor, the homely which has become homeless, as illustrated by the severed eyes in Hoffmann's story, and in the sight that strikes the protagonist, when he in a moment of madness sees death reflected in his beloved's face.

The year following the writing of his essay, Freud returned to the thematic trace of the uncanny, which could only be completed through the experience of profound trauma which struck people, not least as a consequence of the terrors of war. There is, writes Freud in *Beyond the Pleasure Principle*, something demonic in the kind of repetition which does not spring from the return of the repressed, but is the repetition of something which was impossible to repress. Recognising that people in their actions can repeat the most frightening and devastating experiences, and in nightly dreams be haunted by experiences beyond every kind of pleasure, Freud realised that the unconscious is not just the homely and the known, but also the unknown, the demonic and the radically uncanny.

Notes

1 Freud, S. (1920/1976). *Hinsides Lystpricippet. I: Metapsykologi,* bd 2, s. 9–72. København: Hans Reitzels Forlag. Freud, S. (1920): Beyond the Pleasure Principle. *The Standard Edition of the Complete Psychological Works,* Vol. XVIII. London: The Hogarth Press.
2 Freud, S. (1919/1998). *Det uhyggelige.* Købehavn: Forlaget Politisk Revy. Freud, S. (1919). The "Uncanny". *The Standard Edition of the Complete Psychological Works,* Vol. XVII. London: The Hogarth Press.
3 Hoffmann, E.T.A. (1982). The Sandman. In: *Tales of Hoffmann.* London: Penguin Books.
4 Freud, S. (1919). The "Uncanny". *The Standard Edition of the Complete Psychological Works,* Vol. XVII, p. 241. London: The Hogarth Press.
5 Freud, S. (1919). The "Uncanny". *The Standard Edition of the Complete Psychological Works,* Vol. XVII, p. 228. London: The Hogarth Press.
6 Møller, L. (1991). *The Freudian Reading.* Philadelphia: University of Pennsylvania Press.
7 Hoffmann, E.T.A. (1982). *The Sandman.* In: Tales of Hoffmann, pp. 109–110. London: Penguin Books.
8 Winnicott, D.W. (1989/2010). Fear of breakdown. In: C. Winnicott, R. Shepherd & M. Davis (editors) D.W. Winnicott. *Psycho-analytic Exploration.* Cambridge, Massachusetts: Harvard University Press.

Chapter 11

Psychoanalysis at the frontier

Psychoanalysis was never intended as a narrowly restricted specialty for the treatment of individuals with psychic suffering. The unconscious is not bound to repressed ideas and their return in the form of symptoms. It manifests itself in the parapraxes of everyday life, in dreams and wherever human imagination is expressed. Freud was convinced that he had created a method that could also be used outside the clinical field, to uncover the workings of the unconscious in cultural phenomena. His interest in art and literature was propelled by the conviction of the ubiquity of the unconscious, and an indefatigable eagerness to validate the theory of psychoanalysis and its usefulness in areas foreign to the context that had created them.

The most original and insightful results of Freud's science are created at the frontiers of other research areas such as biology, physics and neurophysiology and not least of human sciences such as linguistics, literature and art. A characteristic of Freud's work is that he never hesitated to use models and concepts from other sciences, as long as they threw light on fields that could not be studied empirically, but necessitated uncovering through the means of interpretation, construction and reconstruction. Freud was just as inclined to omit his borrowed material, if more pertinent material came his way. The first attempt to describe the psychic apparatus was formulated on a neurophysiological and purely quantitative basis. When Freud realised the limitations of this approach with respect to the psyche, he gave up the attempt and refrained from publicising his *Project for a Scientific Psychology*. In the same way, he borrowed certain assumptions from biology to justify his conceptualisation of the death drive in the much later text *Beyond the Pleasure Principle*. The nomadic nature of the science of psychoanalysis was propelled by the desire to search for knowledge wherever Freud found traces and manifestations of the unconscious, which he had defined as the object of his science.

The unconscious knows no limits. Nonetheless, it was necessary to delimit a space within which the unconscious could be studied and constructed. The fiction of the psychic apparatus, which Freud created in his interpretation of dreams, and later illustrated in the brief text on the mystic writing pad, became one side of this frame, the setting of the consulting room the other. The boundaries of the consulting room clearly demonstrate the difficulty of containing the simultaneously insistent manifestation of the unconscious as the unknown in the known as well as its inaccessibility. The consulting room is often described as an intermediary area, a potential room and play-ground for free, unbound and mobile psychical processes. One of the fascinating aspects of the work of the psychoanalyst is linked to its dwelling in this intermediary zone, a limbo between wakefulness and dream life, between that which stimulates thought and the mental barriers that halt it. The analytic consulting room was created, on the one hand, with the purpose of laying down necessary limitations for the therapeutic method, with the aim of qualifying it as scientific, and on the other hand, the same room opens for a reality radically different from what lends itself to description in time, space and language. There will always be a gap between what is experienced in the analyst's consulting room and the kind of thinking employed to understand it. We are, in other words, perpetually reminded that the concepts of the functioning of the psychical apparatus are constantly challenged by the encounter with analysands in this very room. This fact has left its mark in the theory and concepts of psychoanalysis, which must, on the one hand, be precise enough to define the essence of the studied phenomena in all their complexity, and on the other hand, possess the flexibility and plasticity necessary to justify these phenomena. In this context, conceptual language often falls short, which is not a coincidence, but a consequence of respect for the complexity and ambiguity of the studied phenomena, since many psychoanalytical concepts are by nature frontier concepts. This applies, not least, to two concepts that have come to play an essential part in the following, where the use of psychoanalysis in the domain of art is discussed. Freud defined the drive as a border concept between the somatic and the psychic, and the concept of sublimation aims to unite processes on the individual and cultural levels.

When psychoanalysis moves away from the well-contained therapeutic setting and its established method of treatment, and puts its method to work in the areas of art and literature, a number of critical questions pertaining to delimitation, relevance and method are opened. Freud's analyses in the domain of art and literature were doubtless motivated by a deeply felt interest, a welcome pause from everyday work in the consulting room and not least by the wish of finding proof for his science outside the clinical field. Freud was in no doubt as to the limitations of psychoanalytic assumptions and explanations regarding subjects such as art and literature, and he was aware of his own limitations concerning the question of what art can offer, and of what the value of art consists.

In his essay *Creative Writers and Day-Dreaming*, Freud writes "we laymen have always been intensely curious to know [...] from what sources that strange being, the creative writer, draws his material, and how he manages to make such an impression on us with it and to arouse in us emotions of which, perhaps, we had not thought ourselves capable".[1] By likening day-dreaming to fantasy, with which psychoanalysis had become familiar through therapeutic work, Freud wished to contribute to the solution of the mystery of the creative writer's sources. This gesture is typical of Freud. On the one hand, he had great esteem for what is also called the artist's secret, and on the other hand, he was convinced that the sources of poetry were the same as those of general imagination. In his detailed study of Michelangelo's *Moses,* Freud concedes to not being knowledgeable in the arts and that his fascination for art was limited by his needing to approach it in his own way. When this proved impossible, as when listening to music or looking at pictorial art, he obtained next to no pleasure.[2] Freud struggled not only with scientific doubts concerning the relevance of psychoanalysis to art, but also with his limitations in enjoying it. Nonetheless, the piece of art through which Freud's analytical method became most famous as well most criticised is a painting, and not just any painting. Leonardo da Vinci's *Mona Lisa* is a painting re-interpreted by artists from Marcel Duchamp to Andy Warhol, who in their painting and photography have attempted to solve the riddle of the wondrous and disturbing smile.

Freud's analysis of Leonardo has, not undeservedly, been held as the prototypical example of the classical psychoanalytical interpretation of art, and critics have focused on the mistakes and flaws inherent in Freud's interpretation, pointing to the insufficiency of the utilised method, which draws upon the artist's biography in the attempt to explain the aesthetic value of the work. However, Freud himself pointed out that his intention was not to explain Leonardo's art, but to uncover the inhibitions of his erotic life and artistic activity. Psychoanalysis cannot explain why Leonardo became an artist, but must limit itself to speak of the significance of these inhibitions for his art. But although Freud clearly draws a limit to what psychoanalysis can approach, he was unable to resist the temptation of touching upon the question of the singular attraction emanating from the *Mona Lisa* and other paintings by Leonardo. He thus pushed the boundary he had himself set down as to the explanatory power of psychoanalysis, when what is in question is beyond the clinical setting. The analysis of Leonardo thus carries its own boundary problematic, so to speak. On the one hand, Freud deploys his analytical method of interpretation, as long as what is in question is the understanding of the childhood memory he found in Leonardo's note-book,[3] and on the other hand. the analysis approaches – if hesitantly – the question of the aesthetic appreciation of art. However, Freud's analysis begins in a place where he felt anchored.

There is a mystery surrounding the person of Leonardo. Increasingly, he turned his interest from art to science, and was, in his artistic work, remarkably slow, at times negligent. Thus, he never finished painting the *Mona Lisa,* and refused to sell it. Leonardo probably did not differ much from other artists, who at times endure painful struggles with their work and can be inclined to flee it. Leonardo exhibited this behaviour to a particularly high degree, writes

Freud. Leonardo also fled intimate and erotic life. While he in his art depicted beautiful creatures emanating a singular, mysterious eroticism, he remained distant to the sexual in his personal life, and his written legacy, which treats the most diverse scientific questions also contain trivial matters which are "chaste and abstinent" and have no relevance to sexuality whatsoever. It is doubtful, concludes Freud, if Leonardo ever embraced a woman or had any intimate relationship with a woman, and as far as we know, his intercourse with beautiful youths did not encompass the sexual. Nevertheless, his passion for research and thirst for knowledge were based on early sexual curiosity, sublimated and cultivated in the unbounded unfolding of the talent for artistic and scientific creation that he possessed. This is Freud's assumption, which encompasses the important idea of sublimation, around which he circulated in many of his writings, but for which he was never able to create a well-defined concept. The analysis of Leonardo would, however, validate the basic assumption that sublimation and the thirst for knowledge depend on an original curiosity in the child concerning the sexual.

Leonardo did not love, nor did he hate, writes Freud. Leonardo has been described as a person whose speculative essence was in harmony with the art he created. "The delicacy of his chiaroscuro, the suppleness of his faces, at times animated with emotion, at others in repose, are the result of meditation".[4] Leonardo's affects were tamed and subjected to the desire for knowledge, but he was not devoid of passion. He transformed his passion into the thirst for knowledge and thus became an illustration of sublimation not being equal to the curbing of passion, but to its unfolding in the service of art. Freud writes of Leonardo that he "had merely converted his passion into a thirst for knowledge; he then applied himself to investigation with the persistence, constancy and penetration which is derived from passion, and at the climax of intellectual labour, when knowledge had been won, he allowed the long restrained affect to break loose and to flow away freely, as a stream of water drawn from a river is allowed to flow away when its work is done".[5]

Leonardo's distant relation to sexuality, combined with his passionate quest for knowledge, gave Freud reason to reconsider the assumption that sublimation consists of a certain de-sexualization, and inspired by the case of Leonardo, he introduced the idea of a third possible way for the sexual researches of children. When the child cannot find the answers to how and why we come to the world, the thirst for knowledge can meet the same fate as the child's infantile sexuality. The quest for knowledge gives way to repression, and is from then on inhibited, and the free working of thinking is restrained. This is neurotic inhibition. In others, intellectual development is strong enough to resist the fate of sexual inhibition, and the drive now lends part of its power to thinking. Research thus becomes a sexual activity, and the researcher loves his quest with the intensity with which others love another human being. The third, and most different, fate, writes Freud, due to its characteristics, evades the inhibition of thinking as well as the neurotic compulsion to think. Sexuality is sublimated into the quest for knowledge, and the drive can act freely in the service of intellectual pursuits. In view of the intense passion for research that was so characteristic of Leonardo, combined with his atrophied sexual life, it is reasonable to think of him as a man who sublimated most of his libido into the passion for research, making it "the core of his nature, and the secret of it".[6]

In this part of his exploration, Freud turns to the childhood memory to which he alludes in the title of his essay. When Freud named his essay *Leonardo da Vinci and a Memory of his Childhood*, he expressed the conscious intention of limiting his study to the experiences gained in clinical work, with his patient's unconscious memories and fantasies. "While I lay in my cradle", writes Leonardo, "a vulture came down to me, and opened my mouth with its tail, and struck me many times with its tail against my lips".[7] Considering that we are dealing with so early a memory, it appears legitimate to regard Leonardo's memory as a later, constructed fantasy, and apply psychoanalytic interpretation to the vulture fantasy. Freud employed literature, mythical and factual knowledge in his attempt to translate the condensed content of the vulture fantasy into a consistent narrative, that could give meaning to the Leonardo case.

I shall not go into the details of Freud's interpretation of Leonardo's fantasy, nor into the mistakes and flaws that critics have revealed. When Freud's interpretation of Leonardo's memory has been refuted on the grounds of historical and linguistic errors of translation, what is overlooked is that it is not factual, historical reality with which Freud is concerned, but its psychic counterpart. Psychic reality is the concept denoting conscious and unconscious fantasy. It is a reality of significations, that invites an interpretative approach. What Freud transfers to the analysis of Leonardo's "memory" are the general laws of fantasy. Accordingly, he assumes the existence of equivalents between Leonardo's memory, latent homosexuality, infantile sexual fantasies and the mythic representation of a phallic mother. Although Freud's references to the significance of the vulture in Egyptian mythology must be withdrawn from his explanation, as he mistakenly translated the Italian *nibbio* to vulture and not to kite, we need not refute his interpretation of Leonardo's "memory". With the addition of new data our interpretation might possibly differ, but this does not necessarily invalidate Freud's analysis of Leonardo's fantasy as revolving around an androgynous vulture. However, what fascinates in Freud's analysis is, to a much further extent, his attempt to approach the question of Leonardo's art and Mona Lisa's mysterious smile.

Leonardo's fantasy moves to yet another level of signification. The peculiar act where the bird opens and closes the boy's mouth must conceal a condensed memory of suckling at the mother's breast and receiving her passionate kiss on the lips. A generous nature, writes Freud, gave the artist the ability to express his earliest and most secret feelings, and in the radiant smile on the long, curved lips, he created a mysterious smile that has disturbed and fascinated viewers for numerous centuries. Never has any artist, writes Freud, "expressed so well the very essence of femininity: tenderness and coquetry, modesty and secret sensuous joy, all the mystery of a heart that holds aloof, a brain that mediates, a personality that holds back and yields nothing of itself save its radiance".[8]

Freud made use of those biographies of Leonardo that were available in his time, and in agreement with these, he points out the ambiguity in Leonardo's paintings, which contain the re-found mother as well as the child Leonardo, depicted as the mother's adored boy. Leonardo's career in art began with depictions of two kinds of objects. The beautiful heads of children can be understood as the multiplication of his child self, and the smiling women as repetitions of his mother, Caterina. Not least, these two figures find their condensed and enchanting expression in *St. Anne with Maria and the Christ Child* "[…] it was his mother, who possessed the mysterious smile – the smile that he had lost and that fascinated him so much when he found it again in the Florentine lady. Thus, it is his mother's smile, he re-creates in his painting, the smile, he had re-found while working on the painting of *St. Anne with Maria and the Christ Child,* and which drove him to create a glorification of motherhood, and to give back to his mother the smile he had found on the noble lady". In conclusion of this interpretation, Freud writes that Leonardo's painting "contains the synthesis of his childhood: its details are to be explained by the most personal impressions in Leonardo's life".[9]

We equally find this mysterious smile in later paintings, depicting male figures. Freud writes on *John the Baptist* and *Bacchus*, that they "[…]do not cast their eyes down, but gaze in mysterious triumph, as if they knew of a great achievement of happiness, about which silence must be kept", and he concludes: "It is possible that in these figures Leonardo has denied the unhappiness of his erotic life and has triumphed over it in his art, by representing the wishes of the boy, infatuated by his mother, as fulfilled in this blissful union of male and female natures".[10] Freud had, in other words, sought to solve the mystery that art critics were unable to solve, and in this context used the theory of the longed-for, desired and lost object. The artist wished to re-find the mother's smile, but also to see himself reflected in the smiling face, which is thus simultaneously the lost object of desire and the desiring subject. In identifying Leonardo's tender and delicate striving for love with the mother's loving gaze, Freud sought to explain the historical fact that Leonardo, in his life and in his painting, preferred beautiful young men with feminine, soft forms. Leonardo's fate was thus identical with that of Narcissus. Both lost themselves in an image coming to them from the outside – Narcissus in his own reflection, Leonardo in his mother's gaze, which he re-found in the figures he created on canvas.

Such is the interpretation within the boundaries of Freud's theory of fantasy, where phenomena are interchangeable. The similarity between the depicted smile and the vulture fantasy is perfect; a common infantile impression has created them. Leonardo strove to reproduce this smile with his paint-brush, and recreated it in all of his paintings.

It is, however, worth noting two words occurring in Freud's description of Leonardo's artistic activity, which helped him both *overcome* the unhappiness of his erotic life and *triumph* over it in his art. These two words point to that which is at stake in the process of sublimation, where the ego stands forth as a creative force and produces something which cannot exhaustively be explained with the help of infantile fantasy. As Paul Ricoeur[11] has shown, sublimation testifies that there is no simple progression from fantasy and the painting when he writes "we can go from the work to the fantasy; we cannot find the work in the fantasy". The creation of art, in other words, entails a transformation, which in Freud's words implies refinement, or elevation. "Their sexual instinct [...] is particularly well fitted to make contributions of this kind since it is endowed with a capacity for sublimation: that is, it has the power to replace its immediate aim by other aims which may be valued more highly and which are not sexual".[12] Ricoeur refers to Freud's famous statement that "where Id was, there Ego shall be", which, applied to Leonardo's vulture fantasy and his art must mean that where childhood fantasies were, there the mother's smile, as work of art, shall be.[13] As far as I can see, this means two things: That the artist sets himself on the side of fantasy, and that he from this place strives to create a highly valued piece of art which transcends the infantile and place-bound character of fantasy. Ricoeur's point is that *Mona Lisa*'s smile does not repeat any real memory. It is neither a question of a memory of the mother nor a memory of the Florentine lady. The Leonardoic smile is a figurative creation seen in relation to every repeated fantasy. The work of art is not limited to exhibiting the object of desire, for the mother's kiss belongs to the mother – the forever lost object – and is in this sense absent. Fantasy is always a replacement for what is absent, only showing its presence on the painter's canvas. The mystery of Mona Lisa's smile is not solved by searching the past for this or that event to be uncovered. We find it in front of ourselves on the painted canvas. The Gioconda's smile undoubtedly takes us back to the "childhood memory of Leonardo da Vinci" but this smile only exists as a symbolizable absence that lies deep beneath Mona Lisa's smile.[14] Although we, on the one hand, acknowledge Freud's assumption of childhood memory as productive in Leonardo's artistic work, we cannot credit it with explanatory power when it comes to the effect the work has on the spectator. In other words, psychoanalysis does not give us the answer as to artistic quality or the effect of work of art on the observer. It is as if something is missing, that could bring us closer to an understanding of the links between those experiences that were productive for the artist, and the creation of the work that expresses this experience. I will try to point out the missing link, by elaborating on the concept of sublimation that was so important in the analysis of Leonardo.

When Freud wrote his analysis of Leonardo, he had not yet introduced his concept of narcissism. With narcissism, the ego gained a whole new significance in psychoanalytic theory, altering the approach to the concept of sublimation. The

re-shaping of sexual activity into a sublimated act, from this point in the development of theory, presupposed an intermediate state, where libidinal energy is
withdrawn into the ego, after which it undergoes de-sexualization and sublimation, thus becoming available for non-sexual activities. The essay on narcissism
also led Freud to abandon his previous differentiation of ego-drives and sexual
drives, gathering them under the term "Eros". This was not just a terminological
renewal, but pointed toward a refinement of the sexual drive, a cultivation of its
very nature. A step was thus taken in the understanding that sublimation is not an
isolated process, but a process that shows that the individual in sublimatory activity
is a part of cultural life. In other words, sublimation is tied to the culture in
question and is itself a cultural process. The transition from sexual and infantile to
erotic and intellectual satisfaction could not take place without the support of
symbolic ideals and the cultural values of an era. But although the ideals of cultural
and social life elicit sublimation, creative energy is freed from the ideals that called
it forth in the process of artistic work. When the painter establishes his love of
sight, the drive energy of sublimation is pure love for what the eye sees, and for
the sensuous and passionate contract between artist and material. Painting, said
Leonardo, is the noblest of the arts, for it serves the eye, "a nobler sense than
hearing, [...] the eye embraces all the fairness of the world".[15] Sublimation, wrote
Freud in his analysis of Leonardo, takes place outside repression. However, this
does not mean, as we noted, that drive energy is given free rein. It certainly means
that censorship is disempowered, but the ego's binding activity entails that the
process of sublimation is to be regarded as a work of culture, as it strives to channel
the untamed drive into the service of culture and Eros.

The concept of sublimation more or less disappeared, along with those of
the drive and the dynamic unconscious, from psychoanalytic terminology
after Freud, in the measure that the self and the object became the basic
matrix of theories of the constitution and development of the psyche. In
the place of sublimation, the idea of reparation, understood as part of the
process of mourning, replaced the concept of sublimation, particularly in
Kleinian interpretations of art and creativity.

I will dwell on the concept of sublimation and attempt to show why it still is
fruitful as the border concept it was intended to be, linking the individual with
the collective and the cultural, retaining the idea of the transformative potential of the drive. Once more, I turn to a famous painting, and with the help
of later theories, add something to Freud's analysis. Sublimation is not restricted to the domain of the ego, which equals an understanding of the
process as a closed circuit in the mind of the artist. Since the drive does not
exist in such a closed circuit, but encompasses the other on its way to gratification, sublimation should also be seen as contingent on the presence of the
other. As Ricoeur noted, Leonardo's childhood memories exist behind *Mona
Lisa*'s smile, but only as symbolised absence. However, more is at stake. The
origin of sublimation, here meaning the origin of the artist's curiosity and
creativity, sends us back to the origin of the sexual drive. Freud's analysis of

Leonardo is one of the rare places where he returns to his long-abandoned theory of seduction. However, it is here a question of maternal seduction. This is to say that it is not only, as Ricoeur seems to imply, a question of memory or representation of the mother. *Mona Lisa* does not refer to the childhood memory, but the artist has in his painting laid down the sexual meaning that the traces of the original situation left behind in the child as a sign he could not, at that point, translate. Traces of the original seduction are found, not least, in the words Freud uses referring to the smile in Leonardo's *Bacchus* and *John the Baptist*. "These pictures breathe a mystical air into whose secret one dares not penetrate [...] the familiar smile of fascination leads one to guess that it is a secret of love".[16] For Leonardo, the "eye is the window of the soul". To this we can add that the soul opens and is opened by the other. Maternal seduction creates in the child a desire that acts as an infinite drive towards intellectual curiosity as well as artistic inspiration. Behind Leonardo's child-hood memory of the bird hides the scene of the child suckling at the maternal breast – a scene that Leonardo, like so many other artists, has rendered as the essence of human beauty. It is in this first contact with the maternal breast, whether real of fantasised, that the apprehension of beauty is created, writes Freud, hereby pointing to the intimate relation between the sexual and the experience of beauty. Also, Rainer Maria Rilke had an eye for the intimate relation between the beautiful, sexuality and the lost object. In *Letters to a Young Poet* he writes: "And indeed artistic experience lies so incredibly close to sexual experience, to its pains and pleasures, that both phenomena are really just different forms of one and the same desire and felicity".[17]

When Leonardo replaced the mother with the bird, we can see it as an expression of the mother's absence – as the loss of the original object of desire and the lack thus constituted in every human child, and not least in the child that is torn from the original object.

For Leonardo, sight was noblest of the senses – a sense that could embrace the beauty of the world, and thus a sense that would prove capable of re-creating the scene that was engraved in his soul. In psychoanalysis as well, sight became a privileged sense. Sight is a drive and is in this context much more than the sensory apparatus we normally equate it to. It is with our eyes we search for what is verbally unavailable, the invisible and forever lost object of desire. I wish to conclude my discussion of Freud's Leonardo analysis by re-ferring to Jacques Lacan's differentiation between sight and the gaze, which was of great importance to his understanding of the perception of beauty.

In his life-long interest in art, Lacan was an insistent proponent that rather than using the method and theory of psychoanalysis on art, we should relate to the work of art in order to study the universal structures of the mind and body, and he was particularly preoccupied with the effects of painting on the viewer. The key to its understanding lies, he claimed, in the relation between the eye and the gaze.[18] Lacan insisted on the pre-existence of a general visibility, beyond every individual's observation of the surrounding world. While the visible world is a world of images, there is a field beyond it for the invisible, and this is the register of the gaze. While sight insists on taking in the world through the magic of images, the gaze strives to make the world symbolically available, which is synonymous with cancelling the eye's appetite for the world's visible aspect. In other words, there is a certain rivalry between the eye and the gaze. What the painter lets us see in his painting is not addressed to the gaze. He gives the eye a tidbit, while simultaneously summoning the spectator to lay down his gaze, as one lays down arms upon entering a church. In this context Lacan writes that this is the fascinating, Apollonian effect of painting. Something is offered – not as much to the gaze as to the eye, which entails that we lower our gaze. What seduces and fascinates when looking at a painting, is a pure and simple displacement of the gaze. At the very same moment, something else appears to be absorbed by the seeing eye.

Notes

1 Freud, S. (1907). Creative Writers and Day-Dreaming. *The Standard Edition of the Complete Psychological Works of Sigmund Freud*, Vol. IX, p. 143. London: The Hogarth Press.
2 Freud, S. (1914). The Moses of Michelangelo. *The Standard Edition of the Complete Psychological Works of Sigmund Freud*, Vol. XIII, p. 211. London: The Hogarth Press.
3 Freud, S. (1910). Leonardo da Vinci and a Memory of his Childhood. *The Standard Edition of the Complete Psychological Works of Sigmund Freud,* Vol. XI. London: The Hogarth Press.
4 Pecírka, J. (1968). *The Drawings of Leonardo and Michelangelo*, p. 11. Middlesex: The Hamlyn Publishing Group.
5 Freud, S. (1910). Leonardo da Vinci and a Memory of his Childhood. *The Standard Edition of the Complete Psychological Works of Sigmund Freud*, Vol. XI, pp. 74–75. London: The Hogarth Press.
6 Freud, S. (1910). Leonardo da Vinci and a Memory of his Childhood. *The Standard Edition of the Complete Psychological Works of Sigmund Freud*, Vol. XI, p. 80. London: The Hogarth Press.
7 Freud, S. (1910). Leonardo da Vinci and a Memory of his Childhood. *The Standard Edition of the Complete Psychological Works of Sigmund Freud*, Vol. XI, p. 82. London: The Hogarth Press.
8 Freud, S. (1910). Leonardo da Vinci and a Memory of his Childhood. *The Standard Edition of the Complete Psychological Works of Sigmund Freud*, Vol. XI, p. 108. London: The Hogarth Press.
9 Freud, S. (1910). Leonardo da Vinci and a Memory of his Childhood. *The Standard Edition of the Complete Psychological Works of Sigmund Freud*, Vol. XI, pp. 111–112. London: The Hogarth Press.
10 Freud, S. (1910). Leonardo da Vinci and a Memory of his Childhood. *The Standard Edition of the Complete Psychological Works of Sigmund Freud*, Vol. XI, pp. 117–118. London: The Hogarth Press.
11 Ricoeur, P. (2012). *On Psychoanalysis. Writings and Lectures*, Vol. I, p. 183. Cambridge: Polity Press.
12 Freud, S. (1910). Leonardo da Vinci and a Memory of his Childhood. *The Standard Edition of the Complete Psychological Works of Sigmund Freud*, Vol. XI, p. 78. London: The Hogarth Press.

13 Ricoeur, P. (2012). *On Psychoanalysis. Writings and Lectures,* Vol. I, p. 183. Cambridge: Polity Press.
14 Ricoeur, P. (1970). *Freud and Philosophy. An Essay on Interpretation,* pp. 173–174. London: Yale University Press.
15 Pecírka, J. *The Drawings of Leonardo and Michelangelo,* p. 19. Middlesex: The Hamlyn Publishing Group.
16 Freud, S. (1910). Leonardo da Vinci and a Memory of his Childhood. *The Standard Edition of the Complete Psychological Works of Sigmund Freud,* Vol. XI, p. 117. London: The Hogarth Press.
17 Rilke, R. M. (1929/2011). *Letters to a Young Poet,* p. 41. New York: Harvard University Press.
18 Lacan, J. (1973/1998). The split between the eye and the gaze, pp. 67–78. In: *The Four Fundamental Concepts of Psychoanalysis. Seminar XI.* New York: W.W. Norton & Co.

Index

For Product Safety Concerns and Information please contact our EU
representative GPSR@taylorandfrancis.com
Taylor & Francis Verlag GmbH, Kaufingerstraße 24, 80331 München, Germany

www.ingramcontent.com/pod-product-compliance
Lightning Source LLC
Chambersburg PA
CBHW070347270326
41926CB00017B/4024